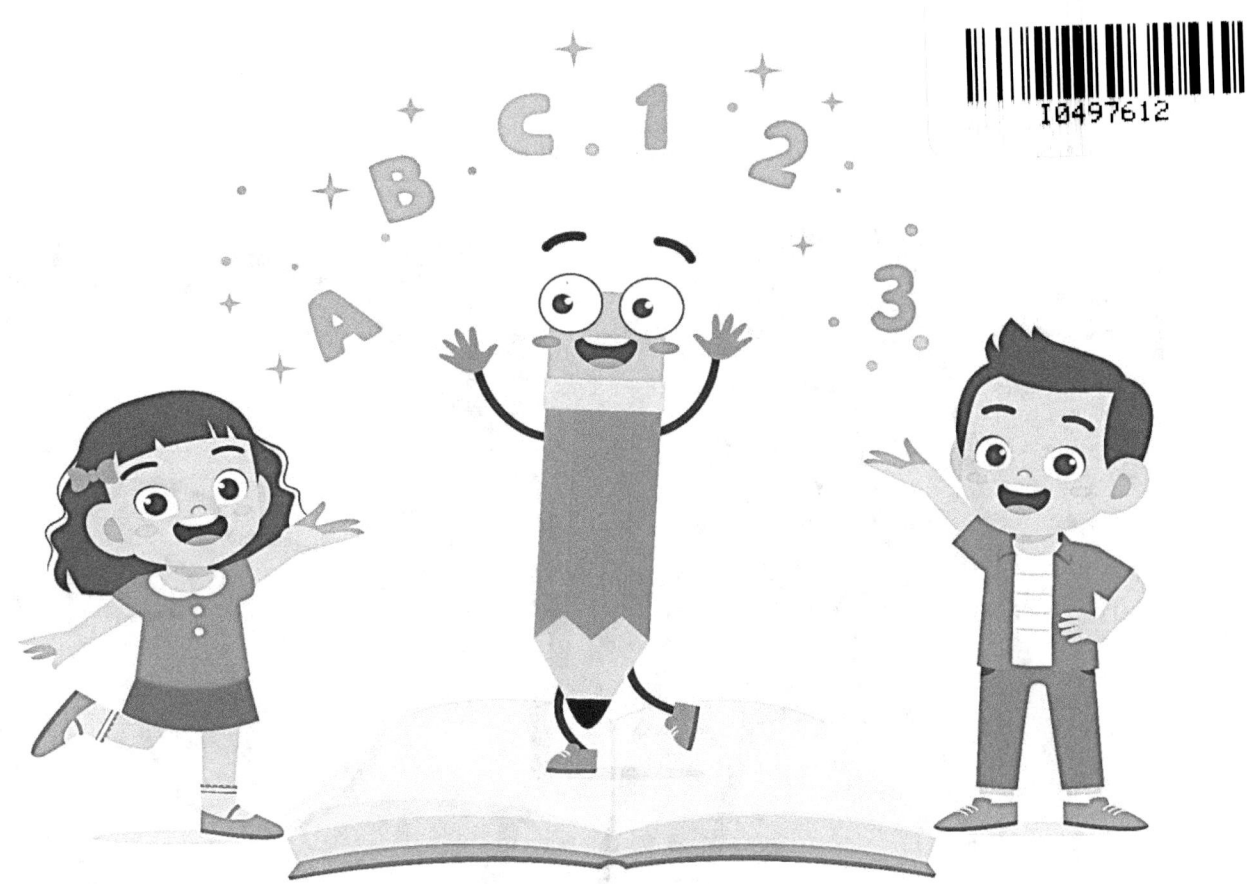

Email us at
francisko.janka@gmail.com

to get free extras

just titre the email –**A to Z Coloring** -
And we will send some extra
surprises your way

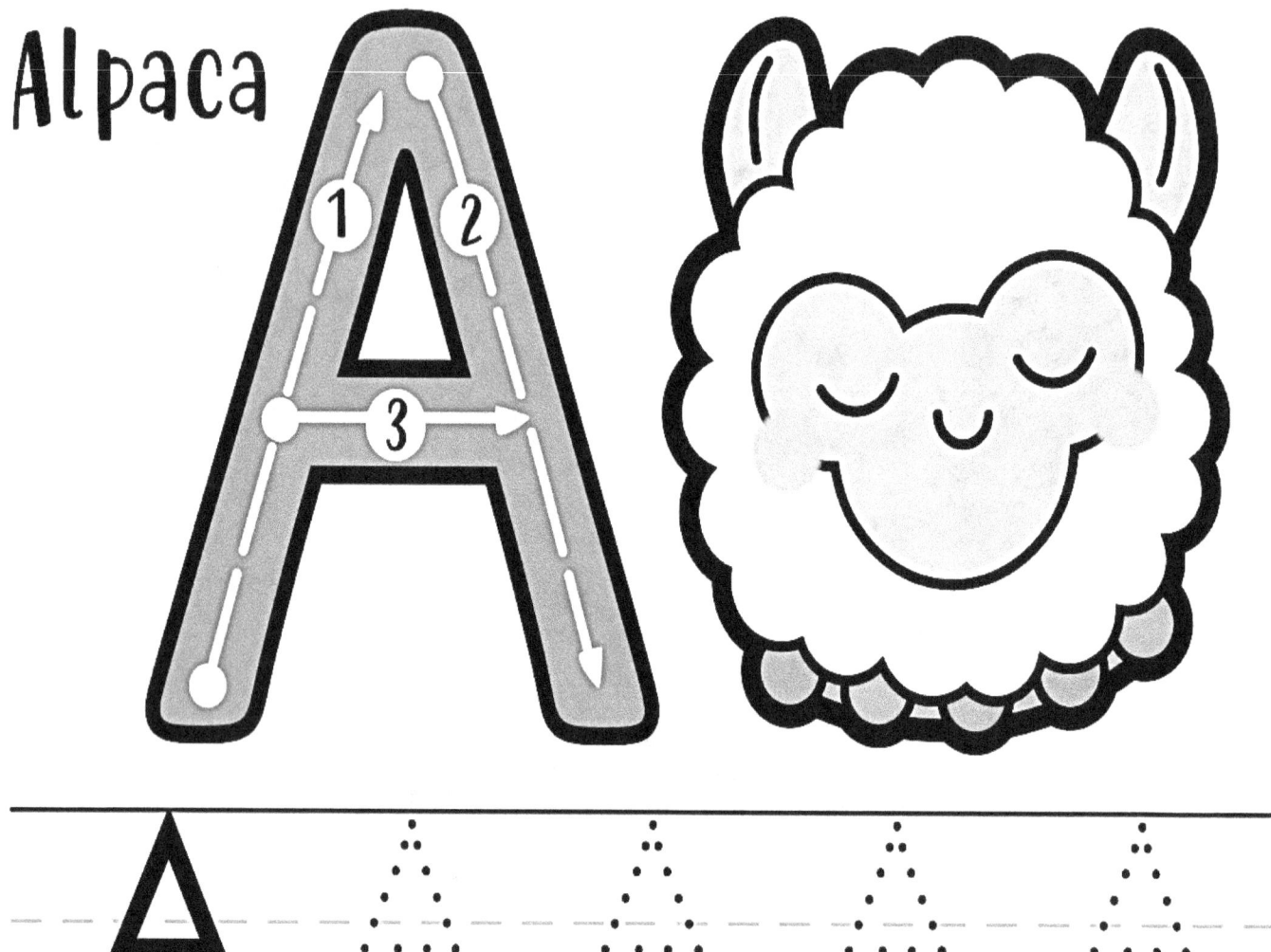

Trace & Color Letters

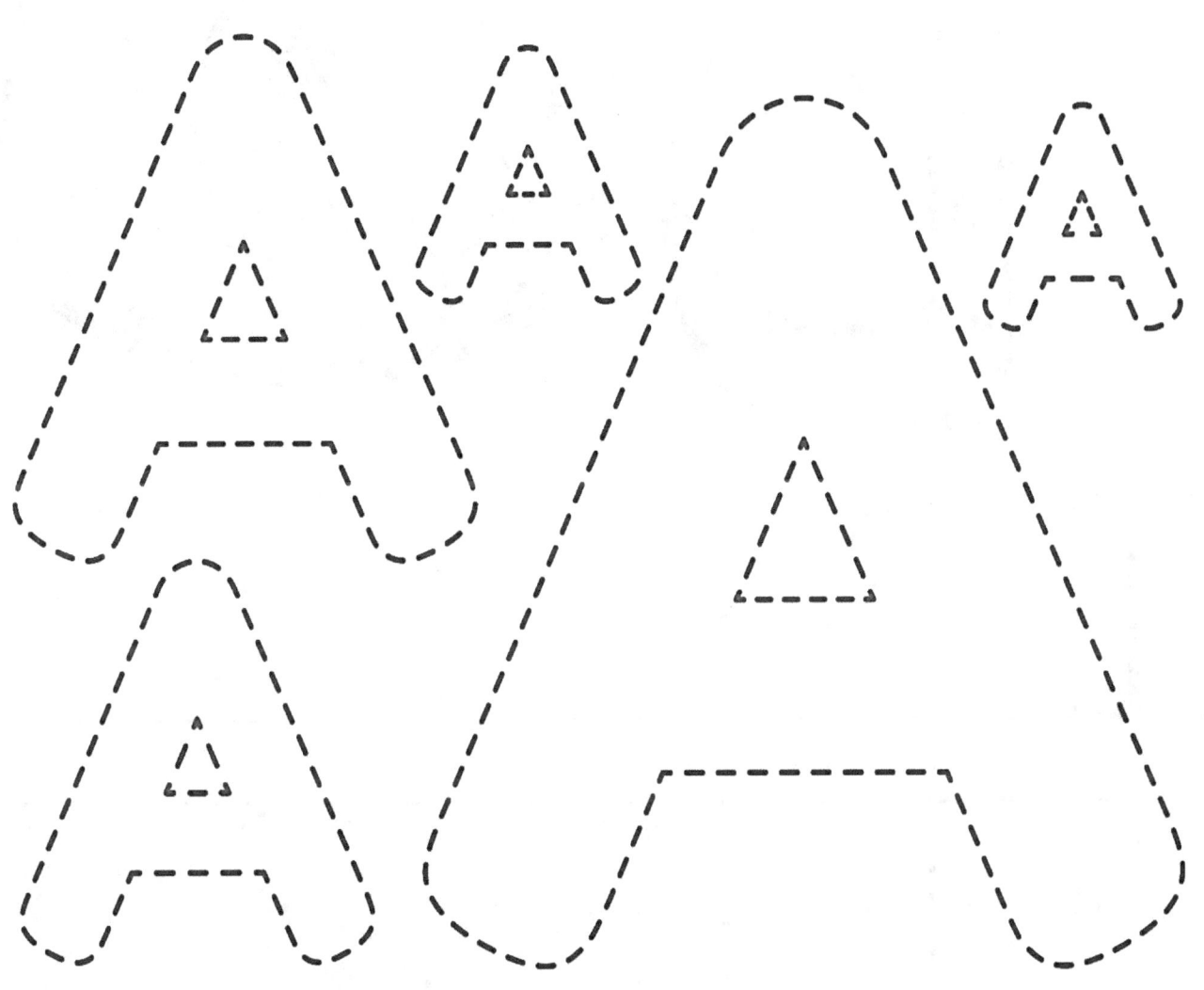

Bear B

B B B B B B

B B B B B B

Trace & Color Letters

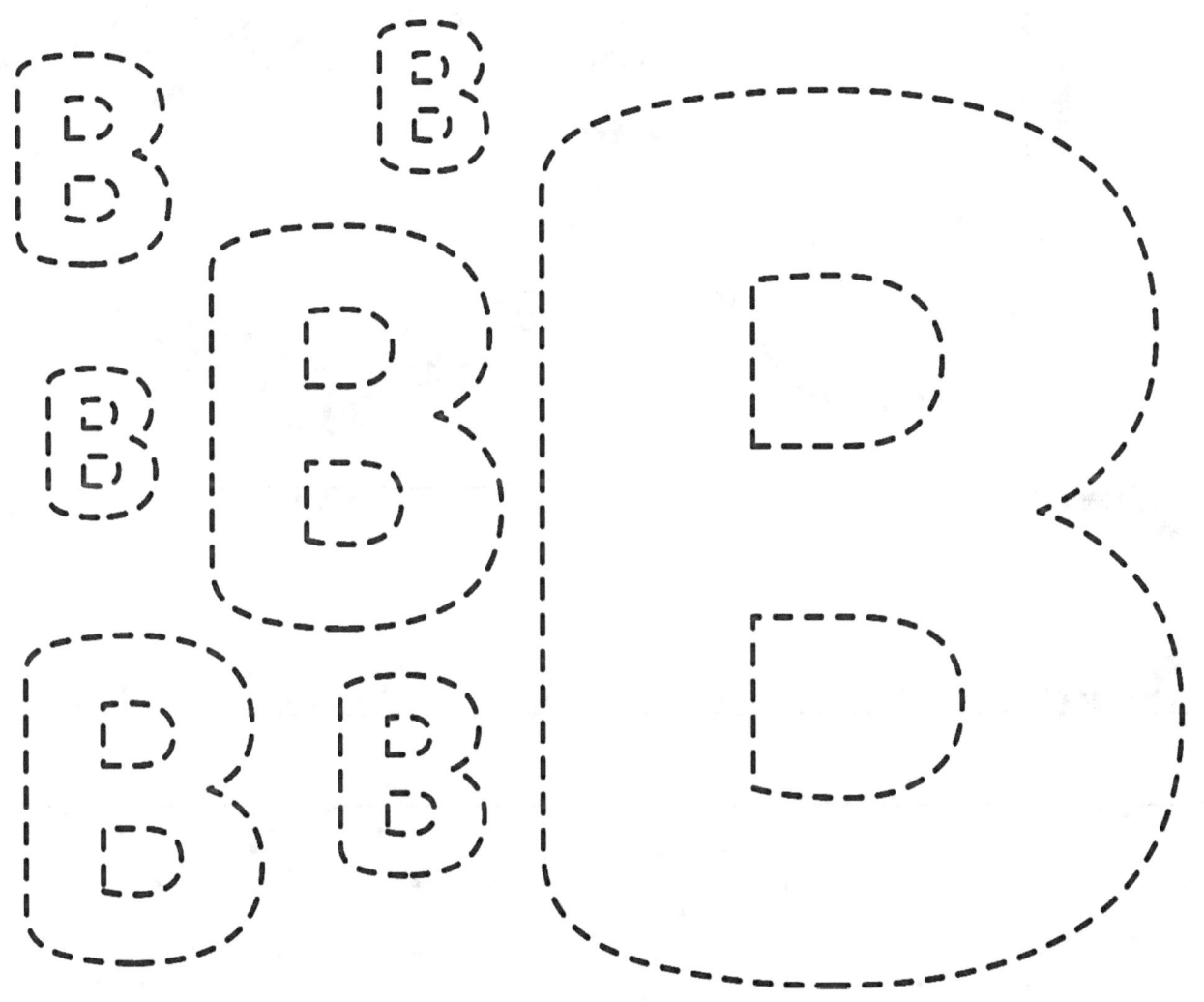

Cat

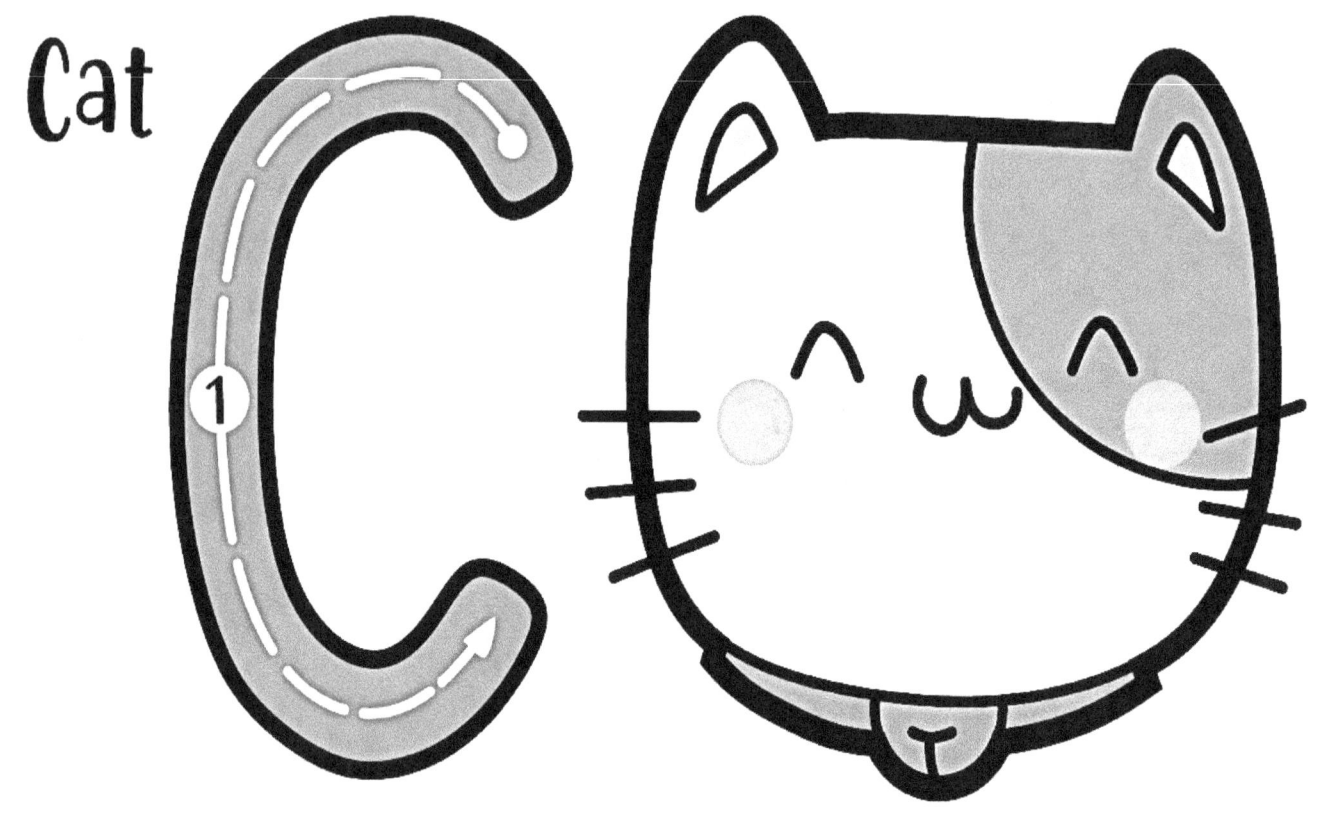

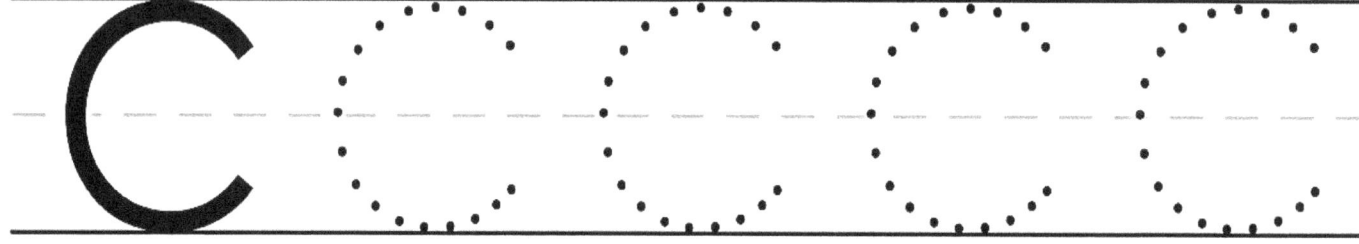

Trace & Color Letters

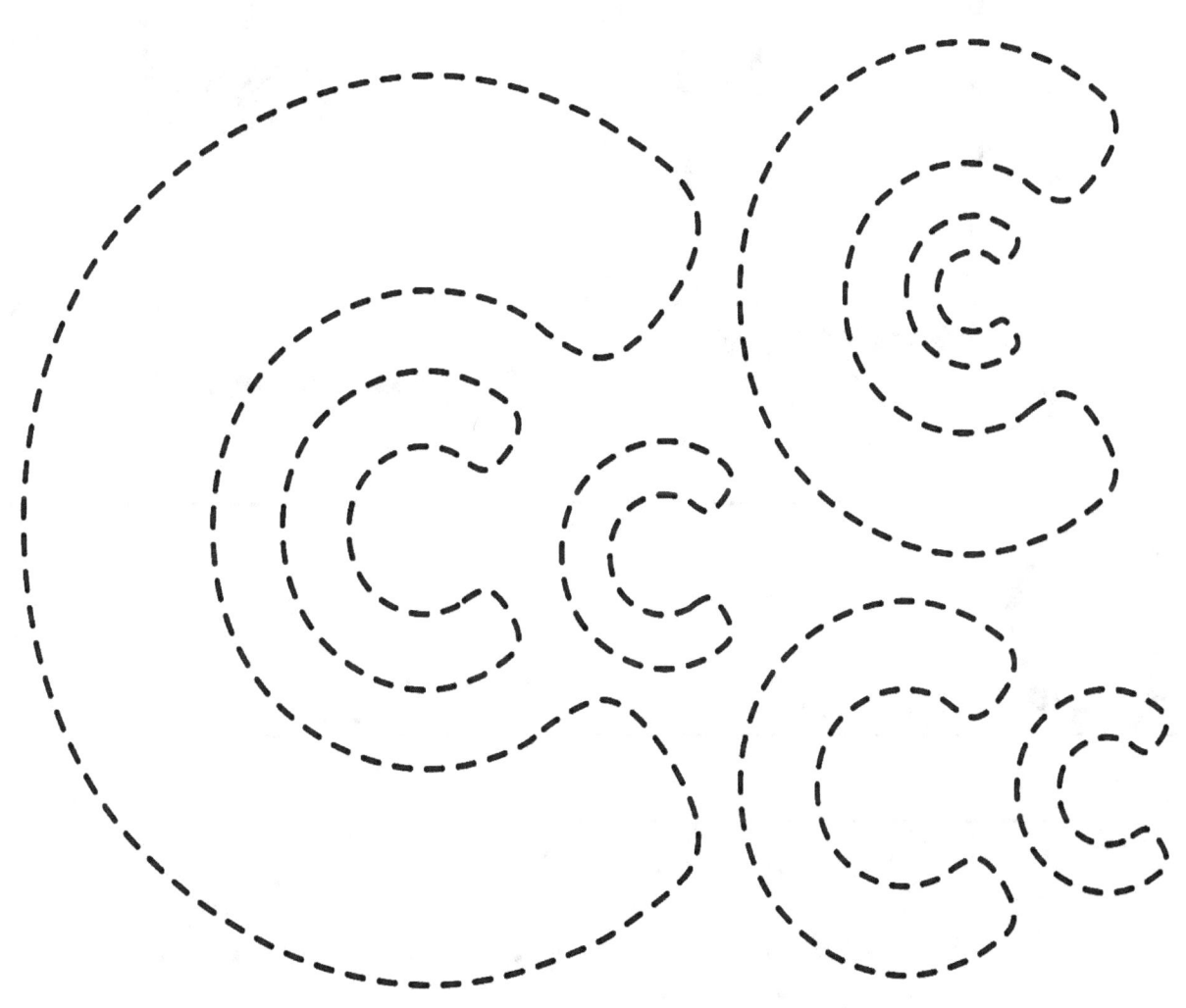

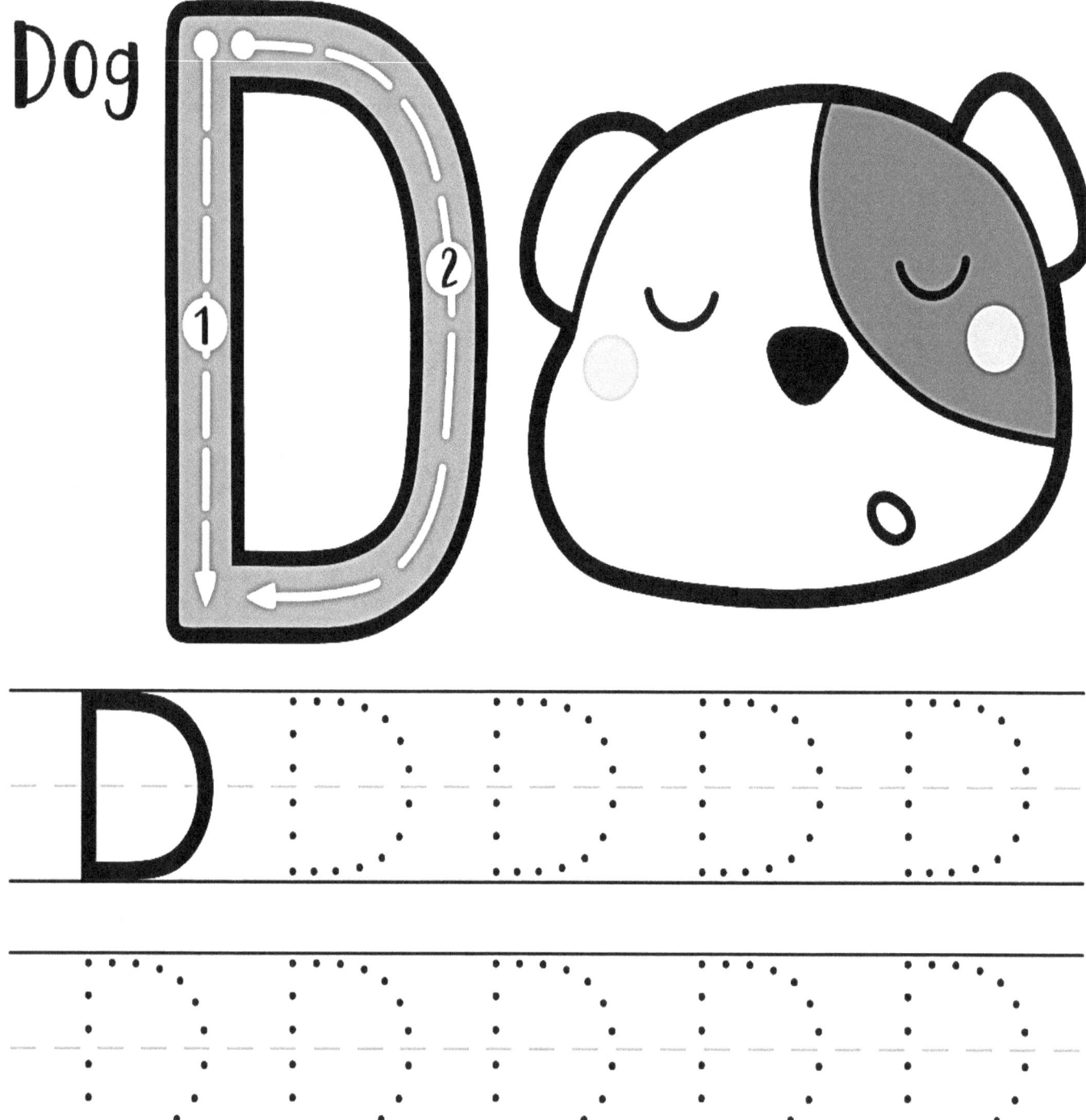

Trace & Color Letters

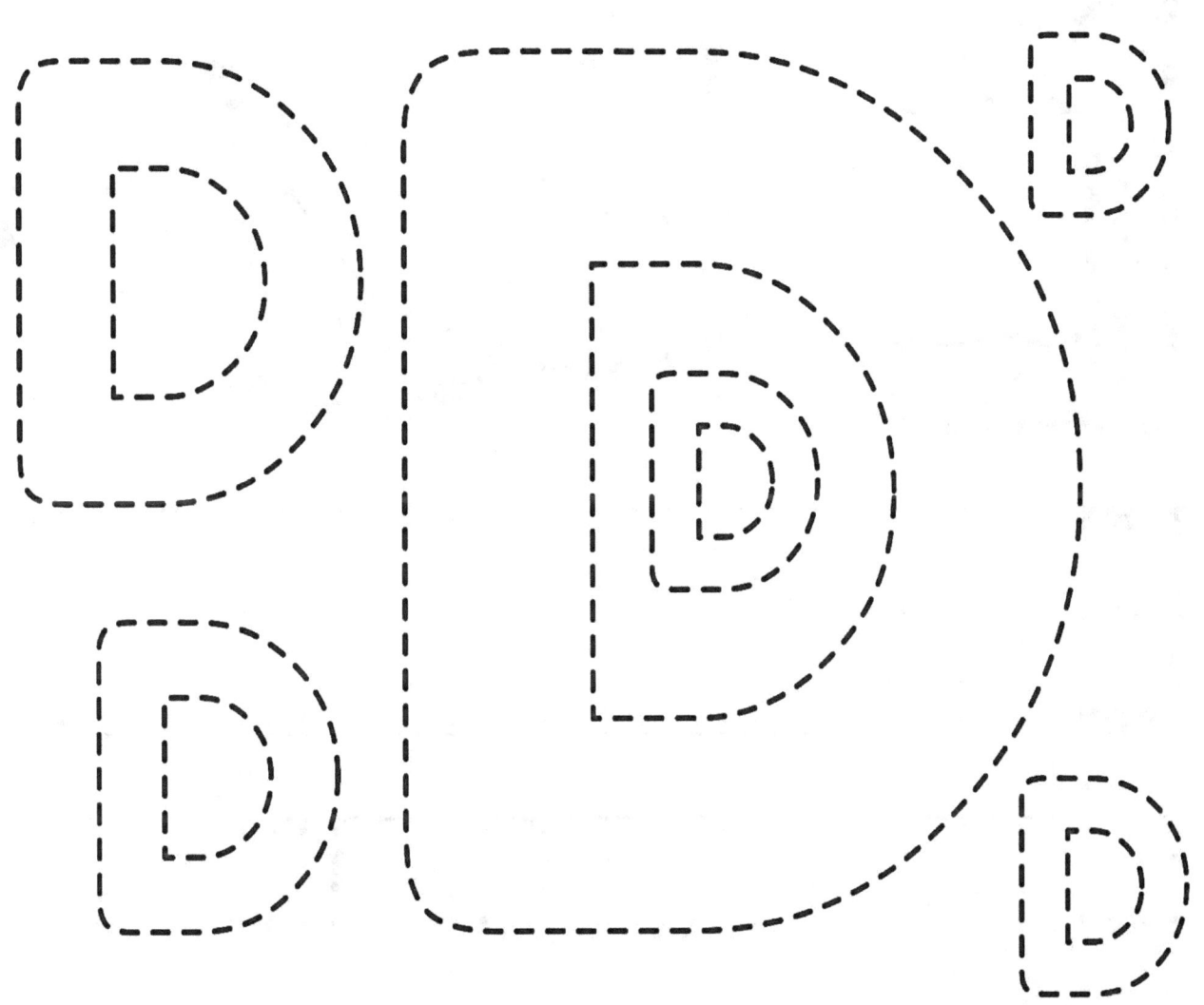

Elephant

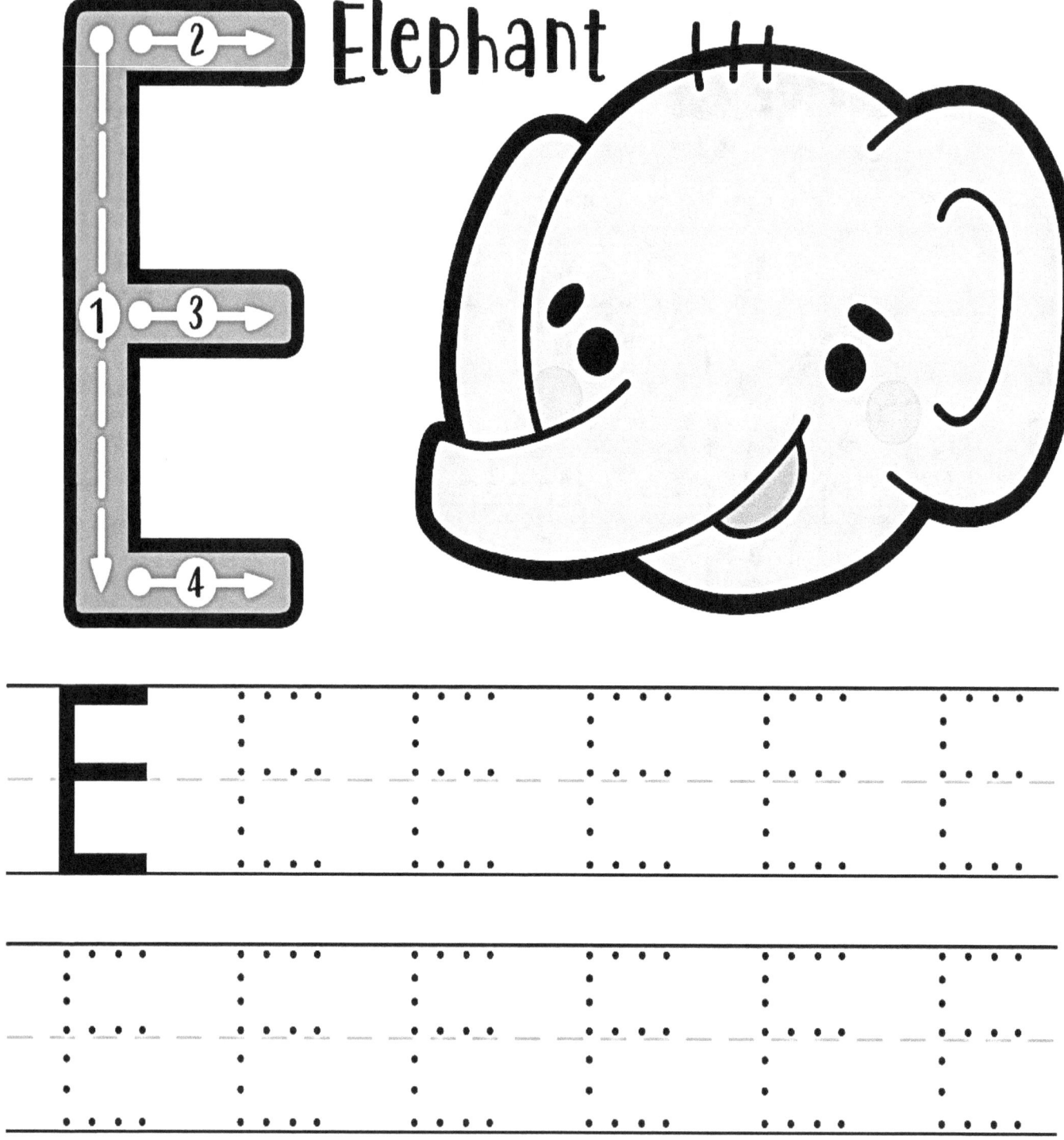

Trace & Color Letters

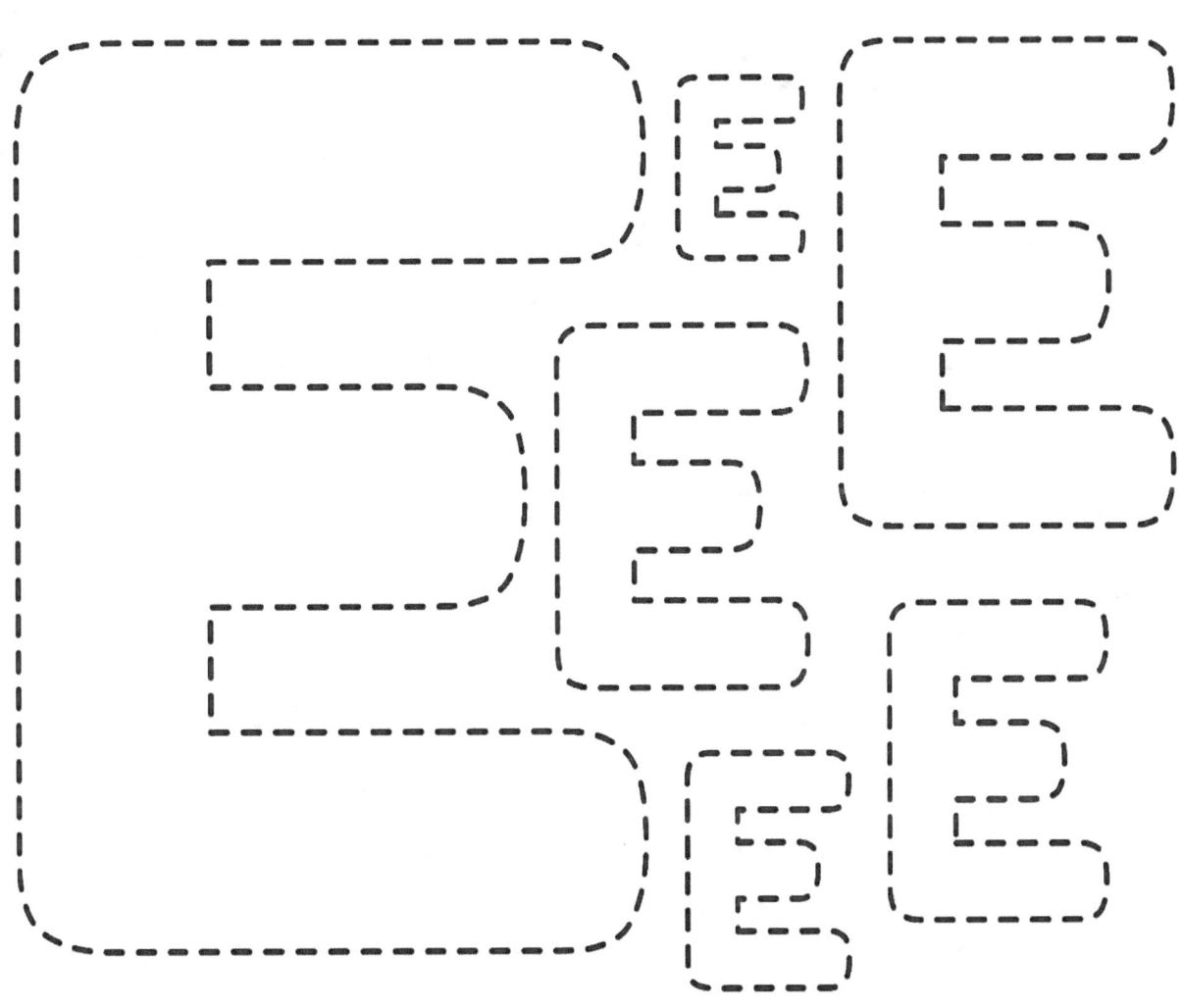

Frog

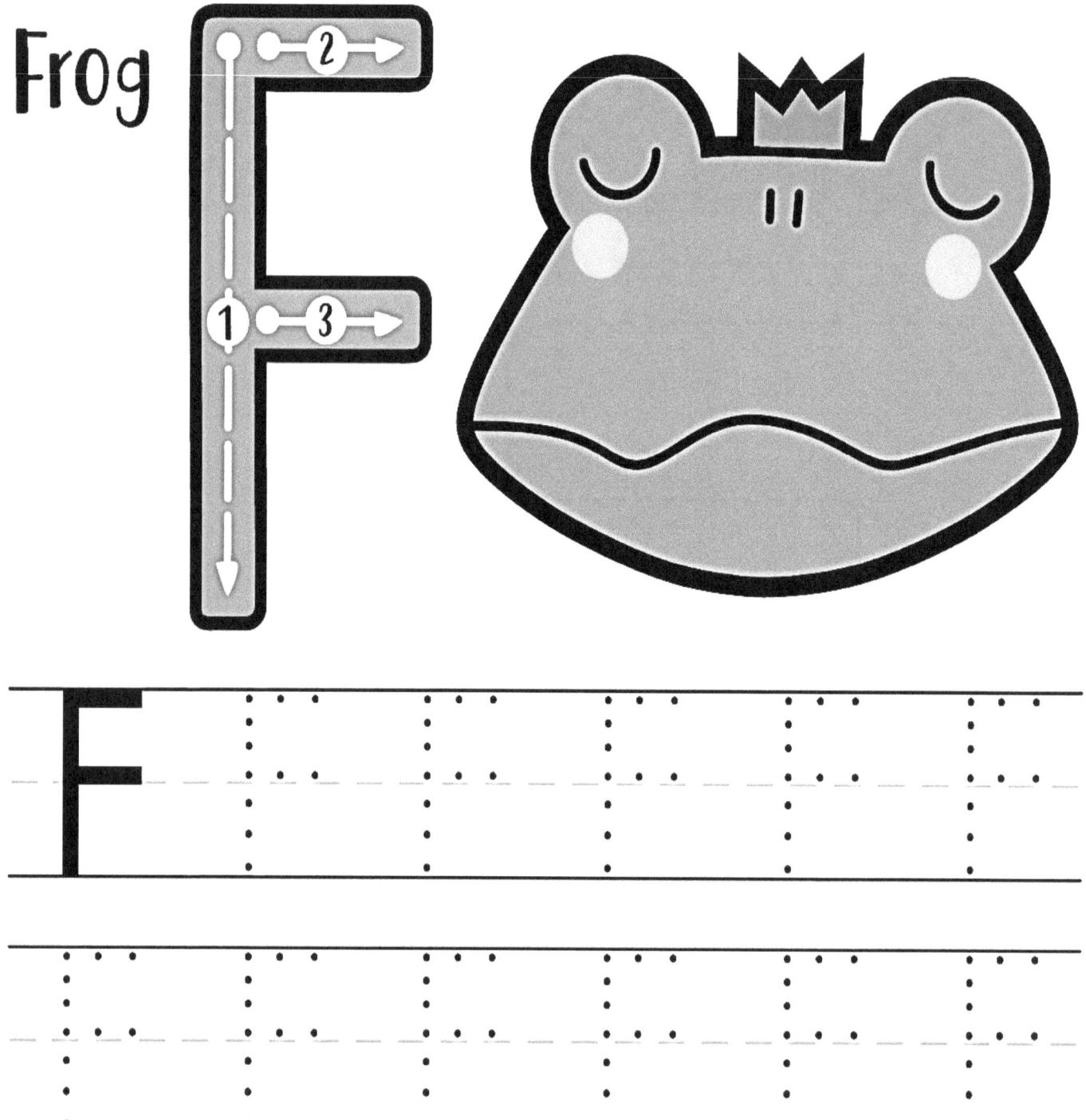

Trace & Color Letters

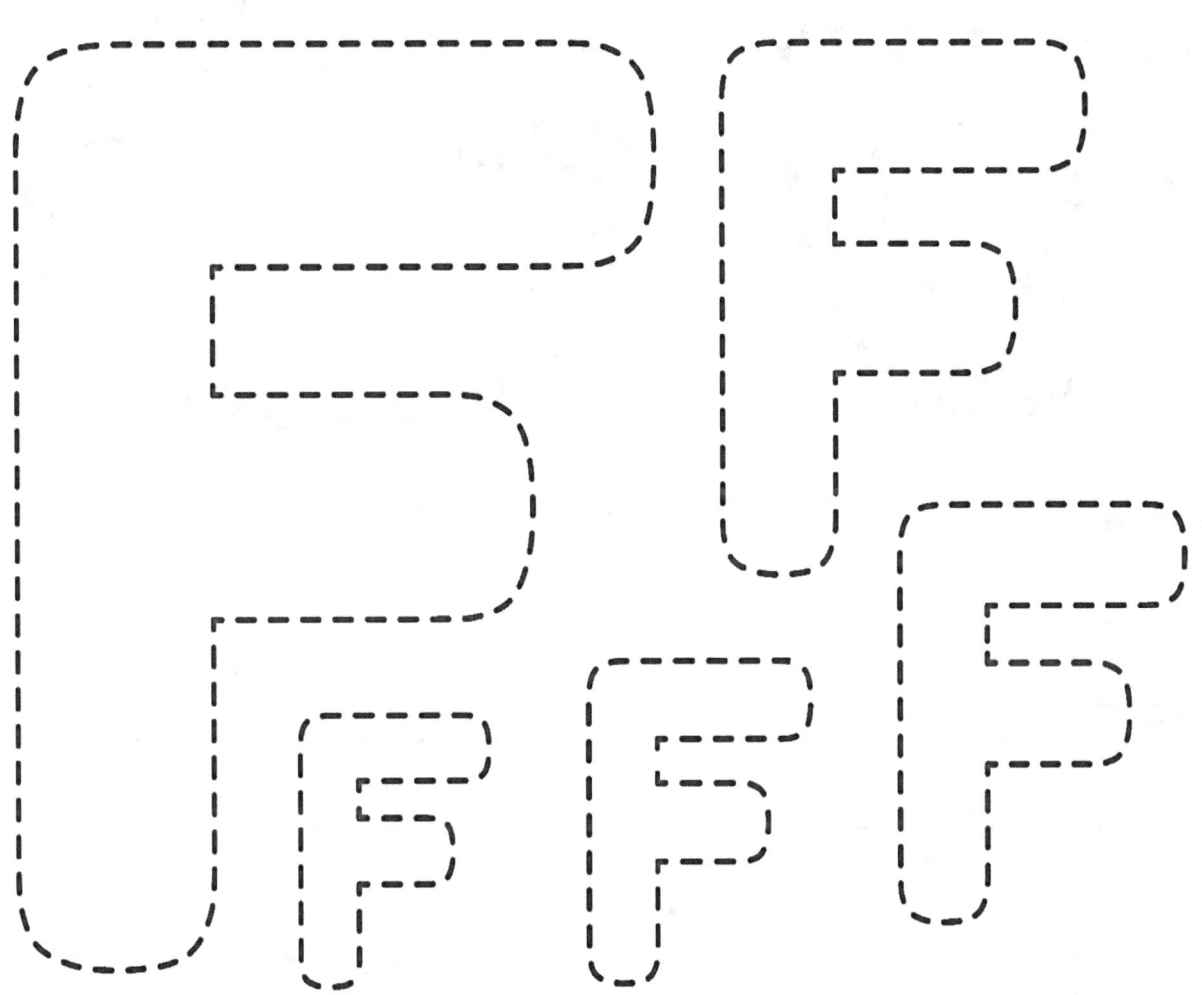

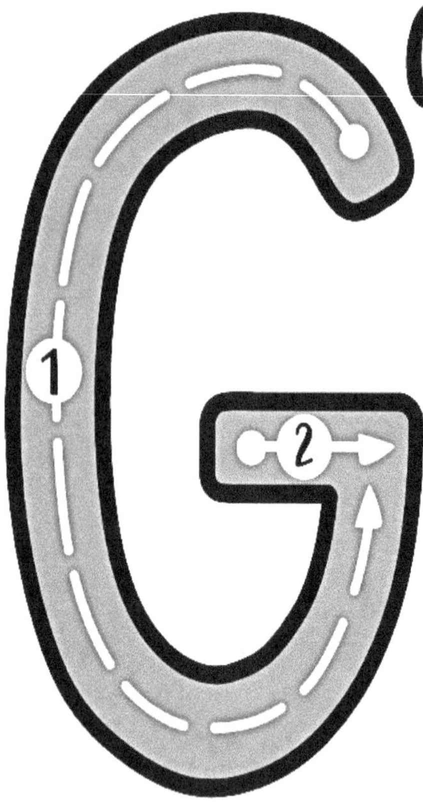

Giraffe

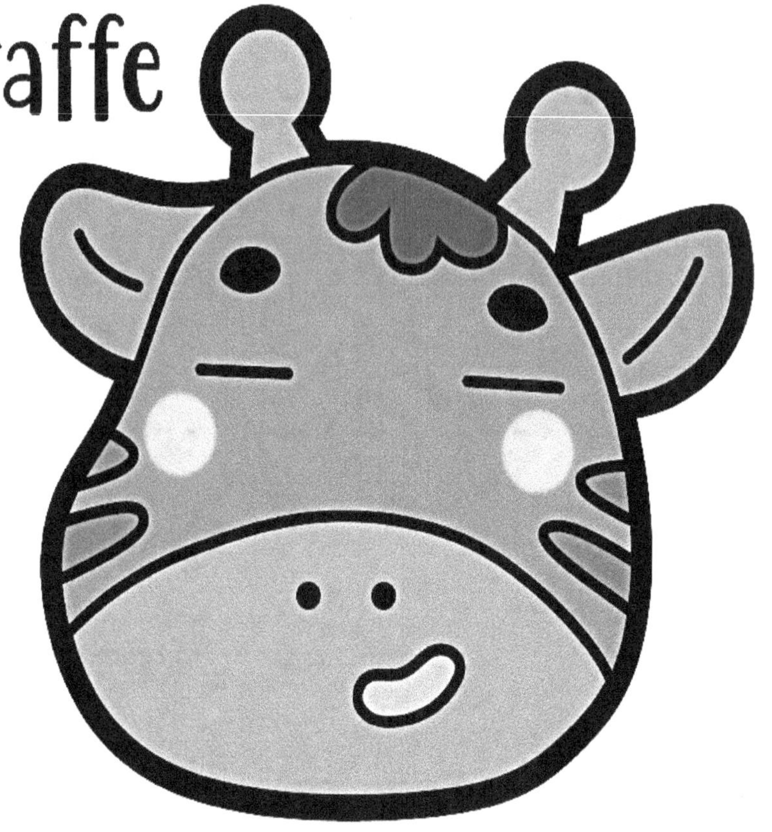

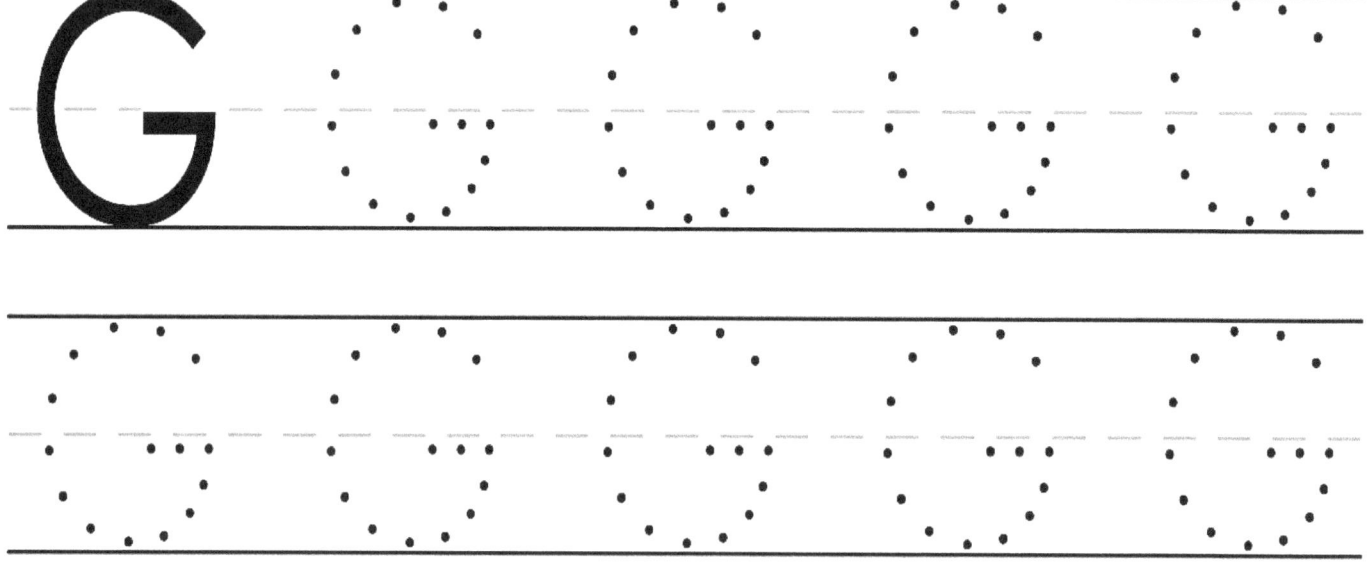

Trace & Color Letters

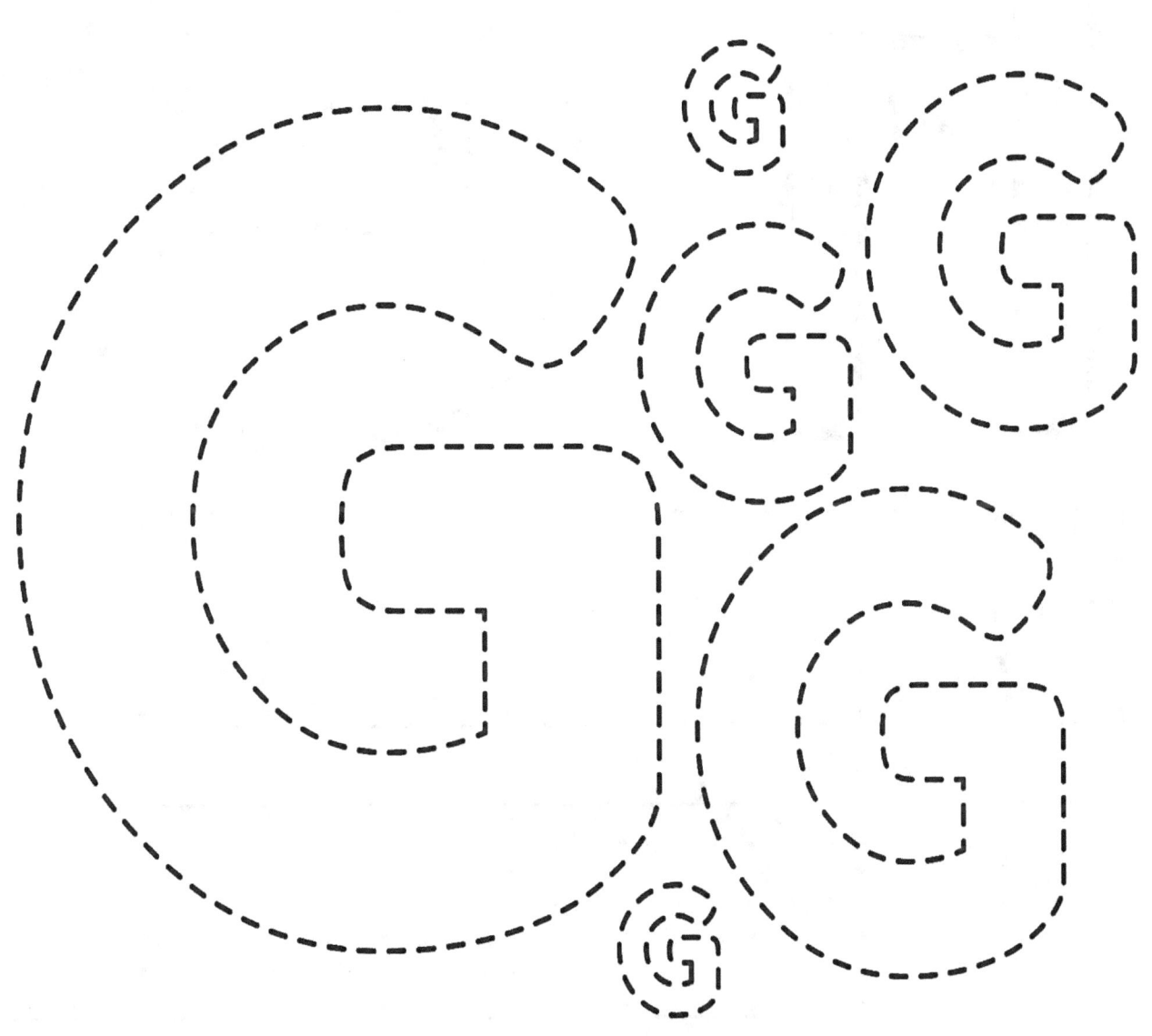

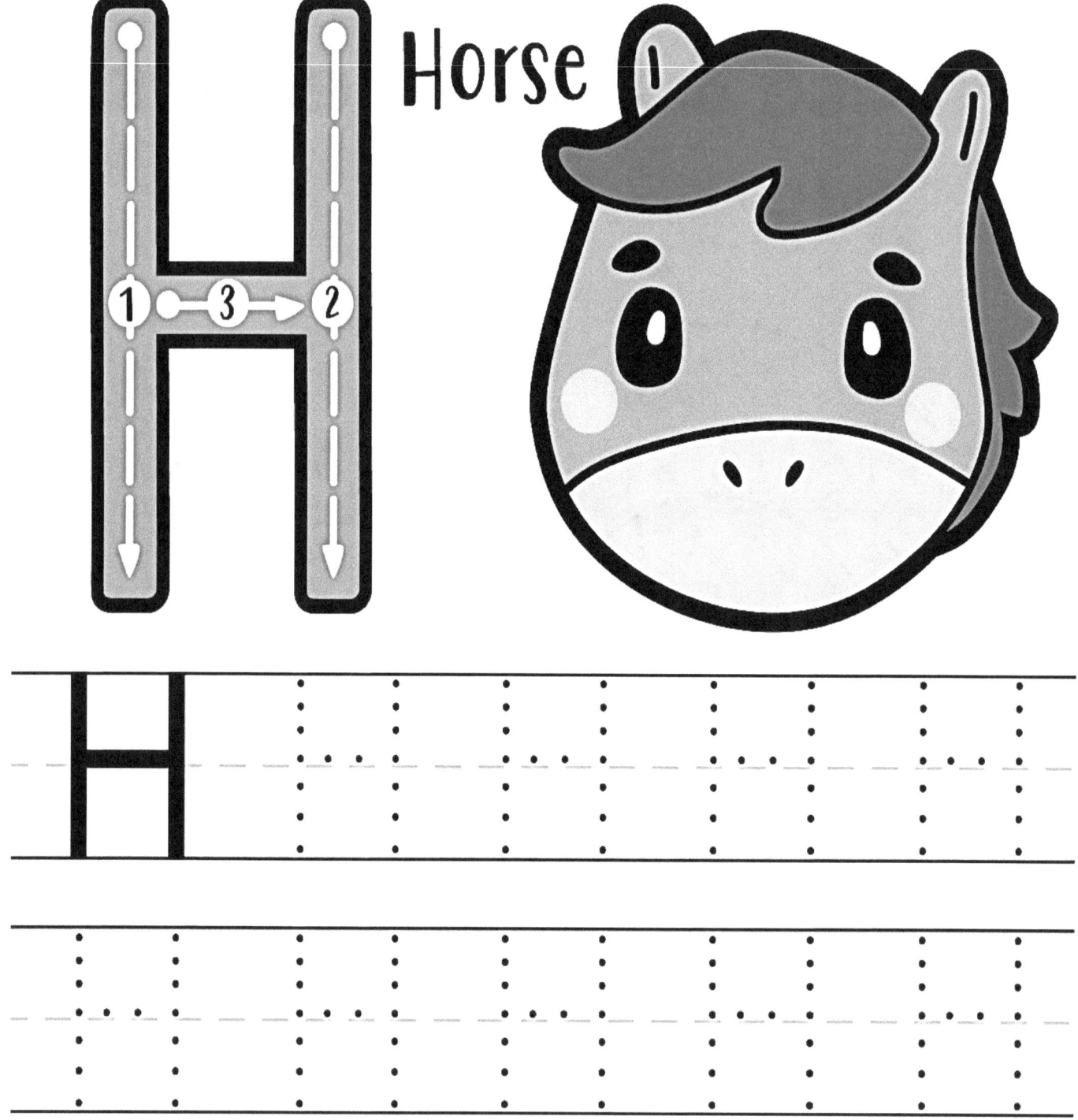

Trace & Color Letters

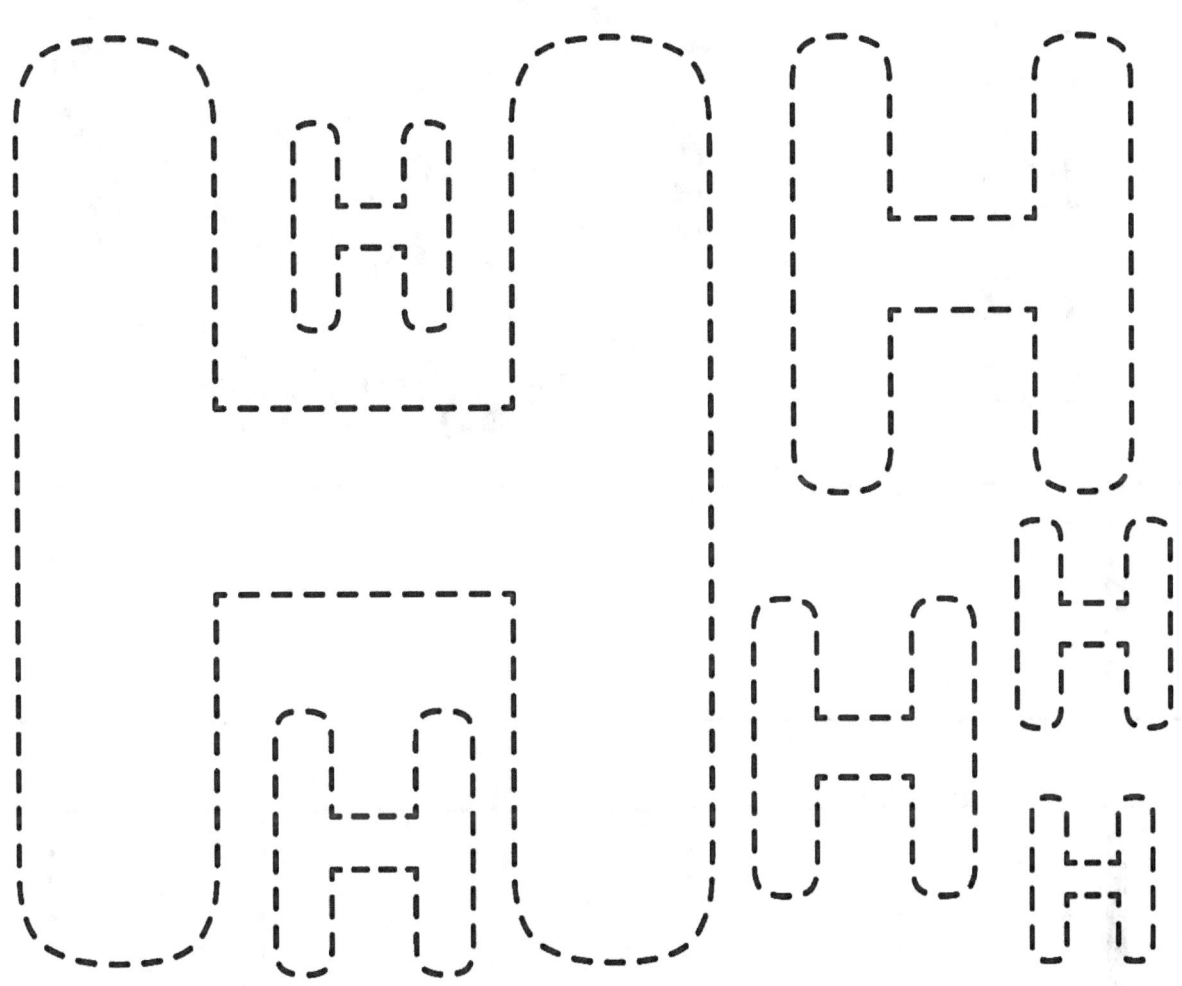

Iguana

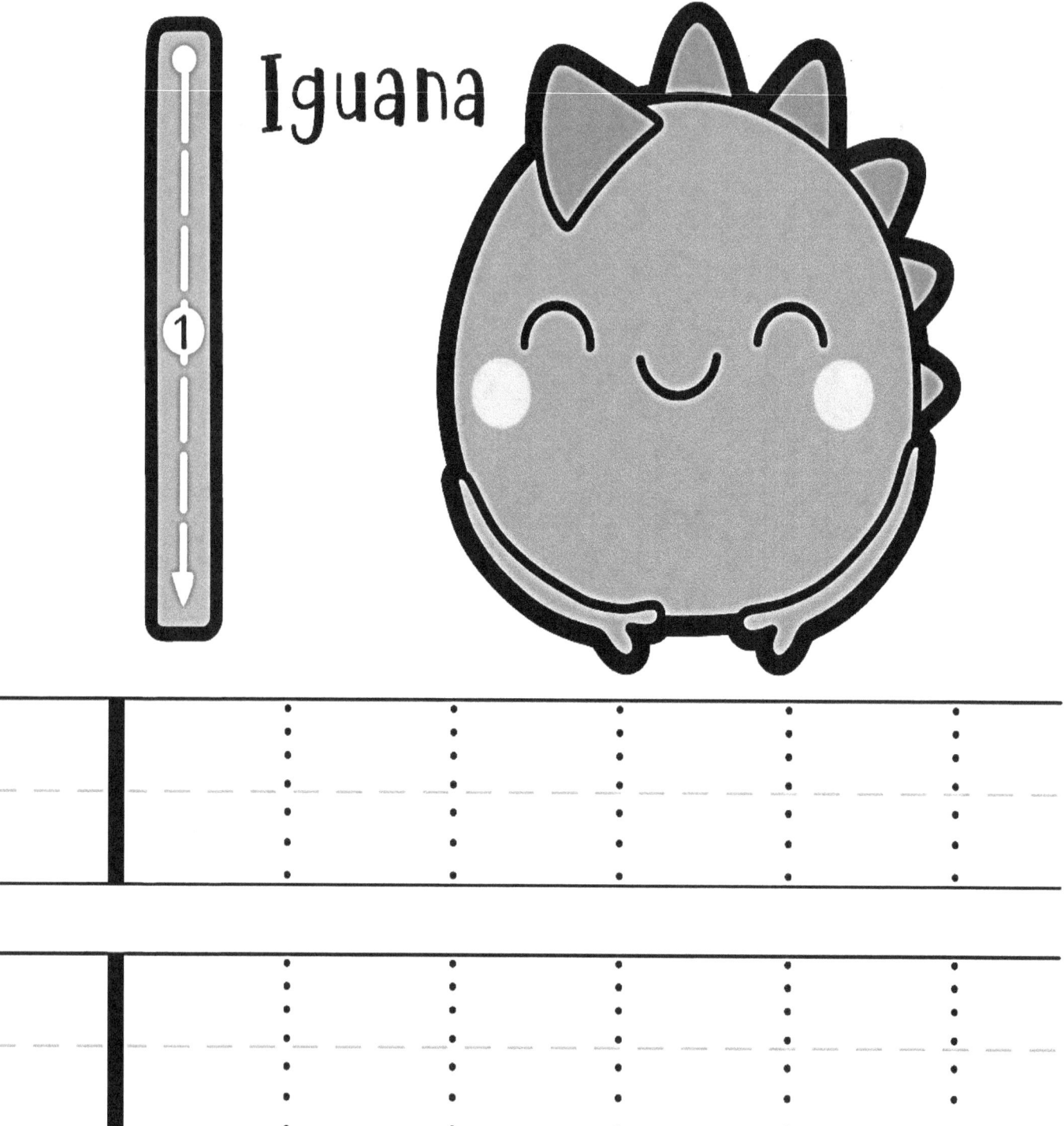

Trace & Color Letters

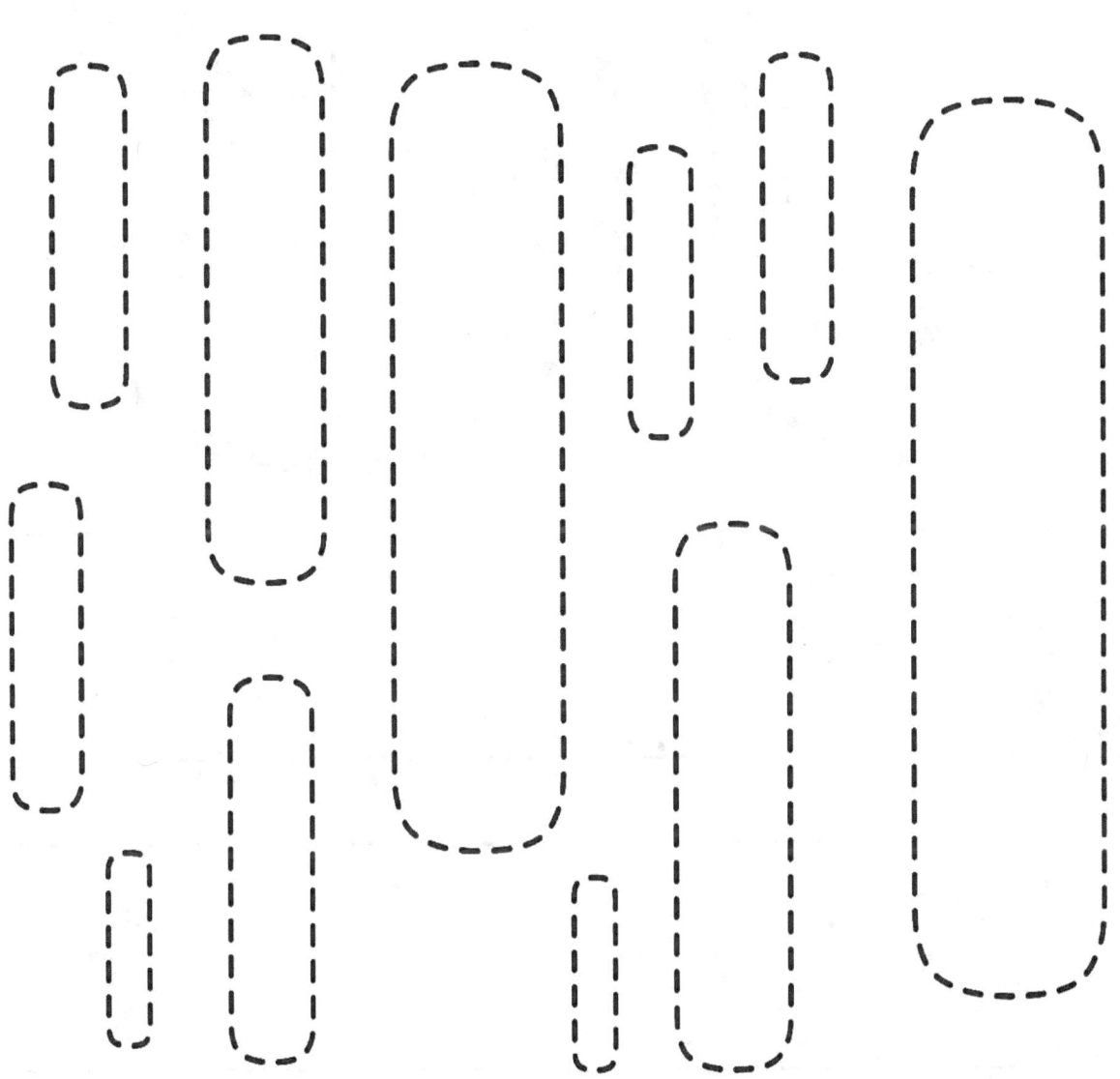

Jaguar

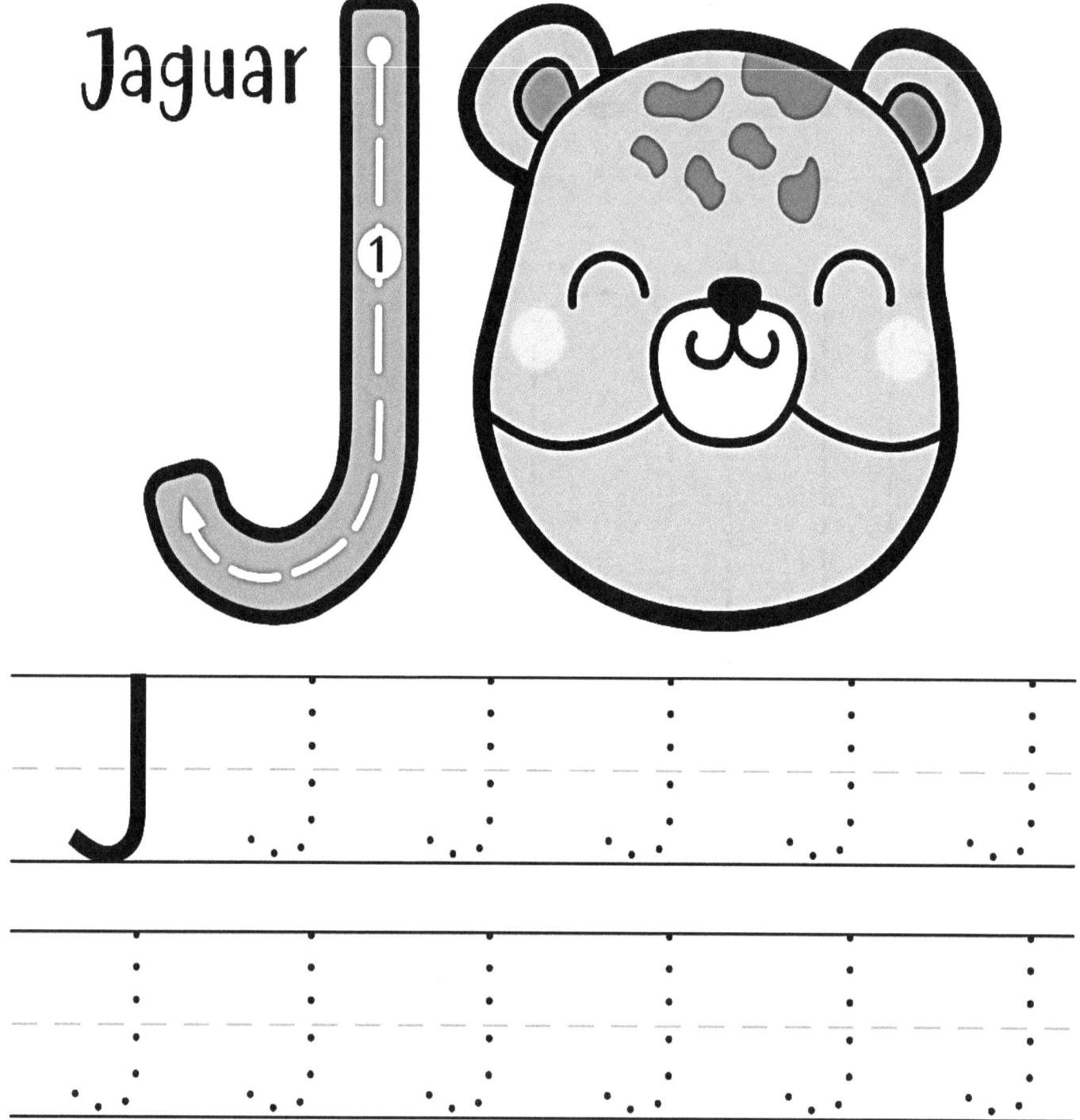

Trace & Color Letters

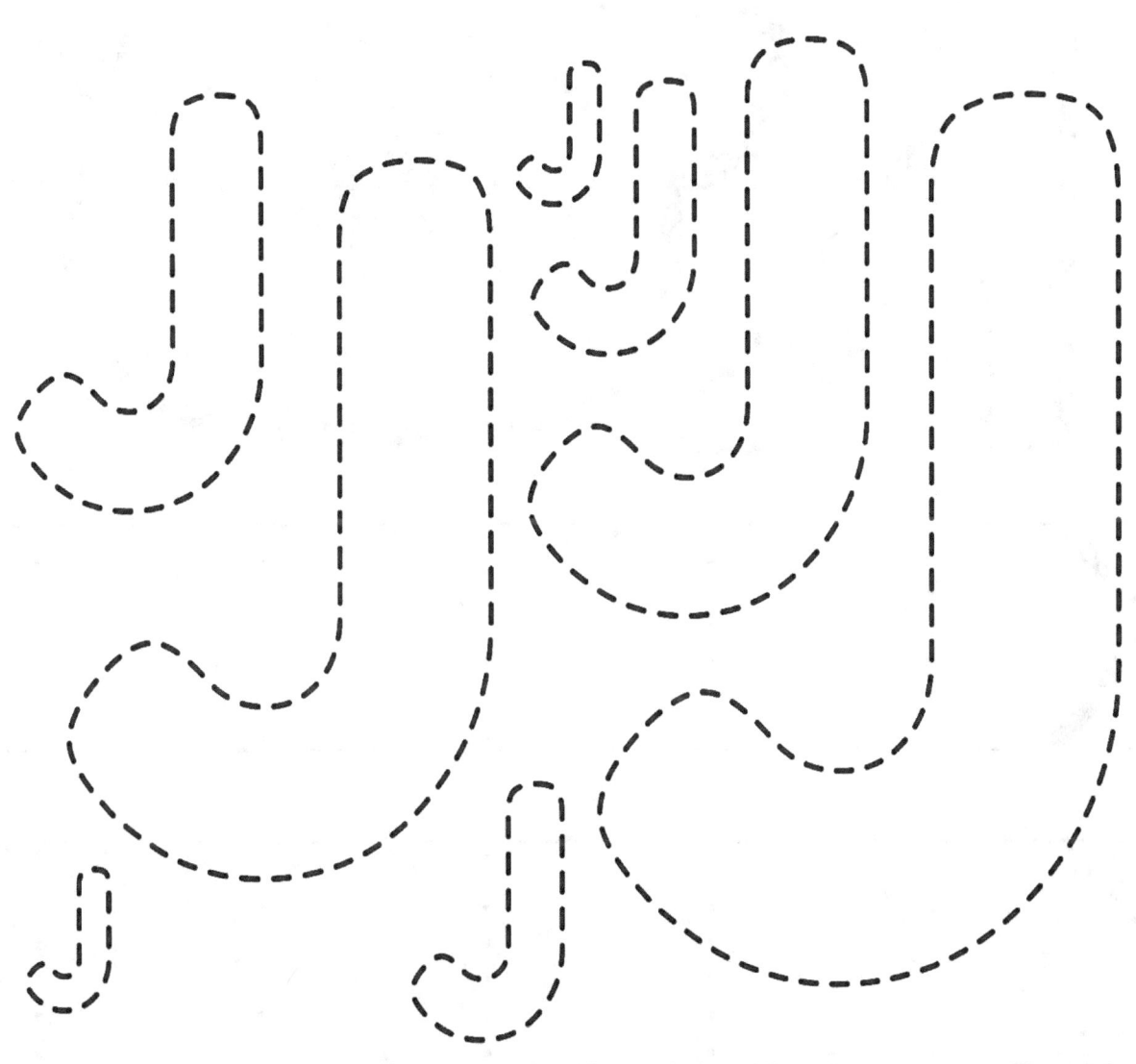

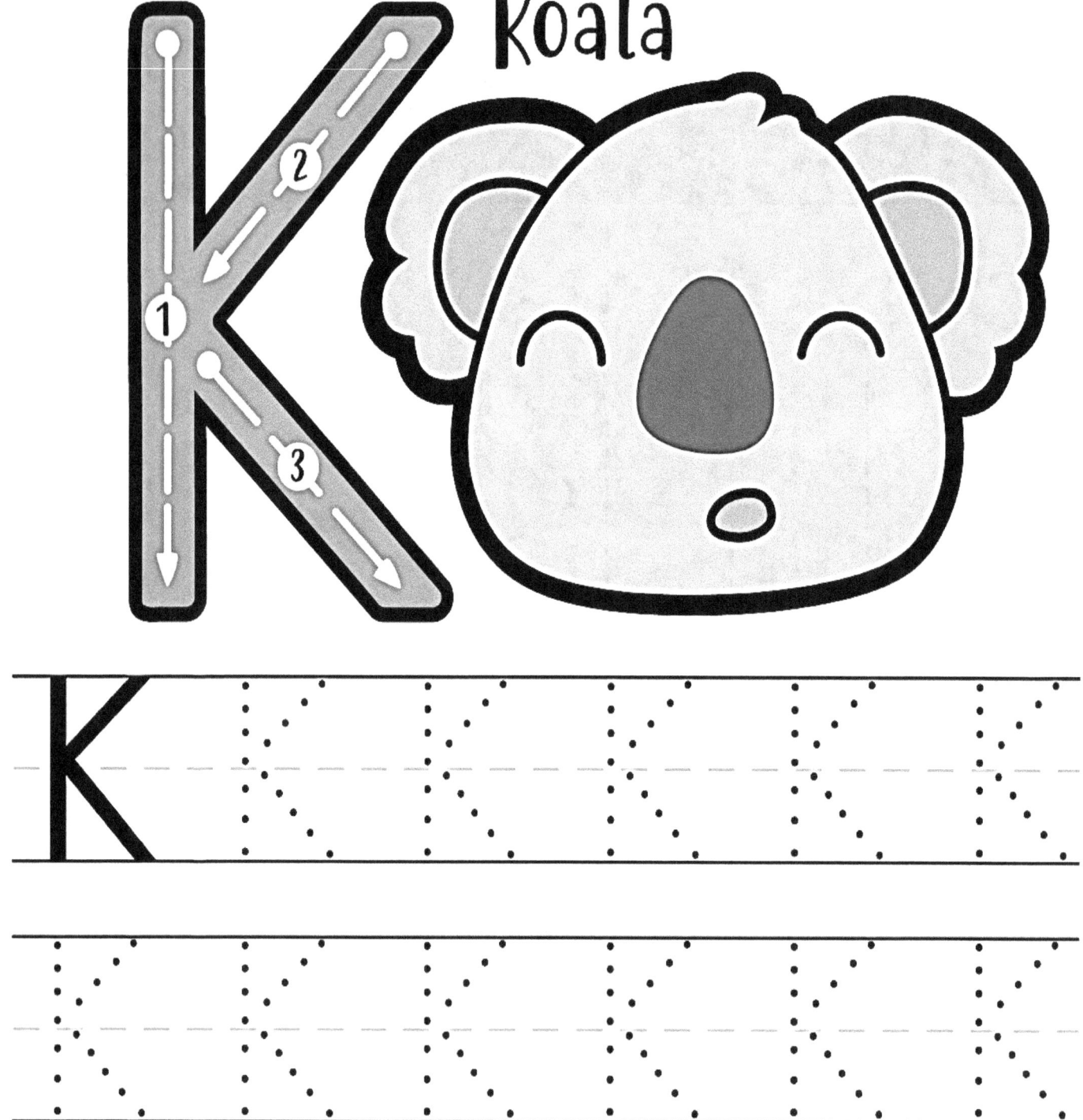

Trace & Color Letters

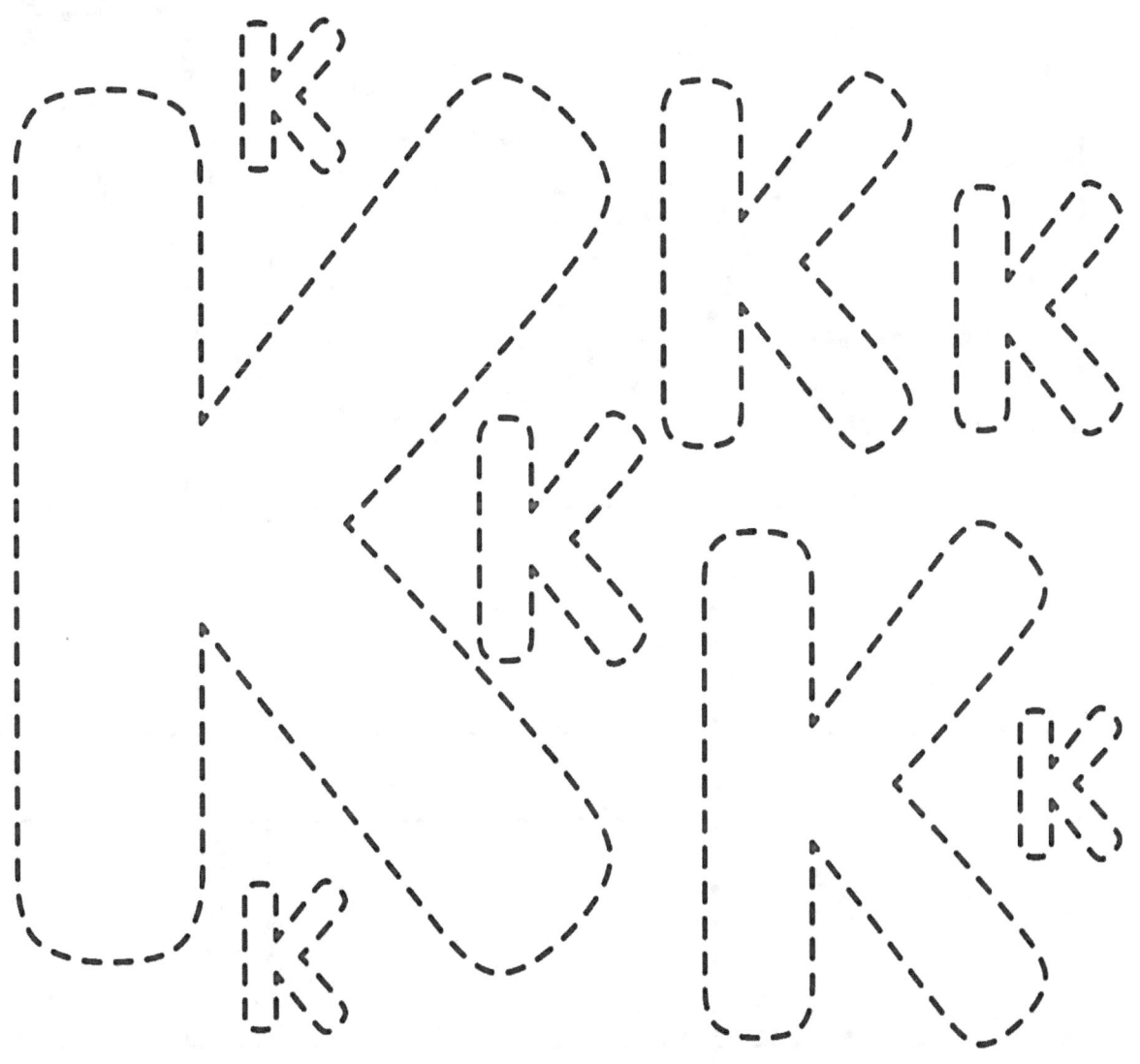

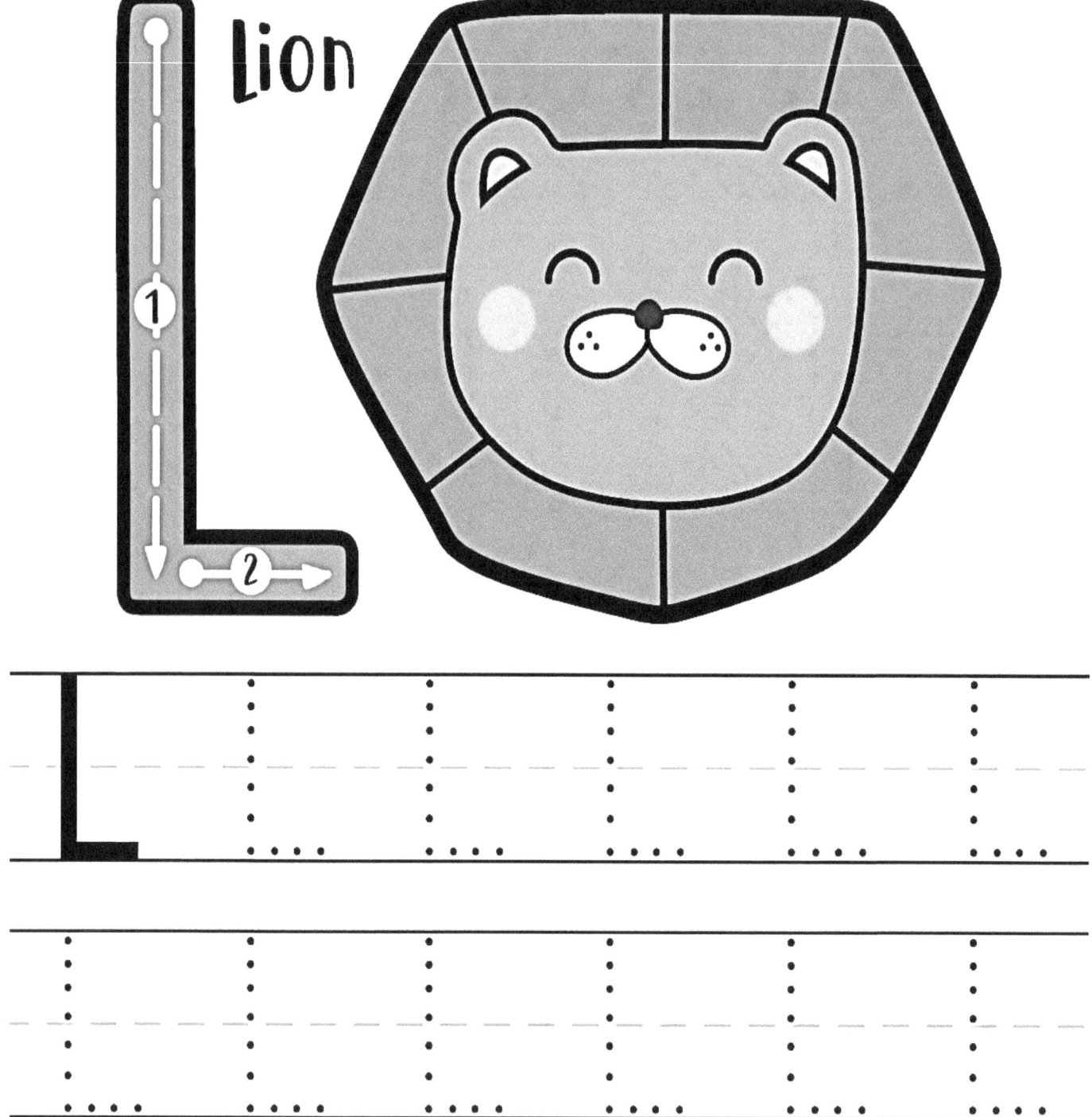
Lion

Trace & Color Letters

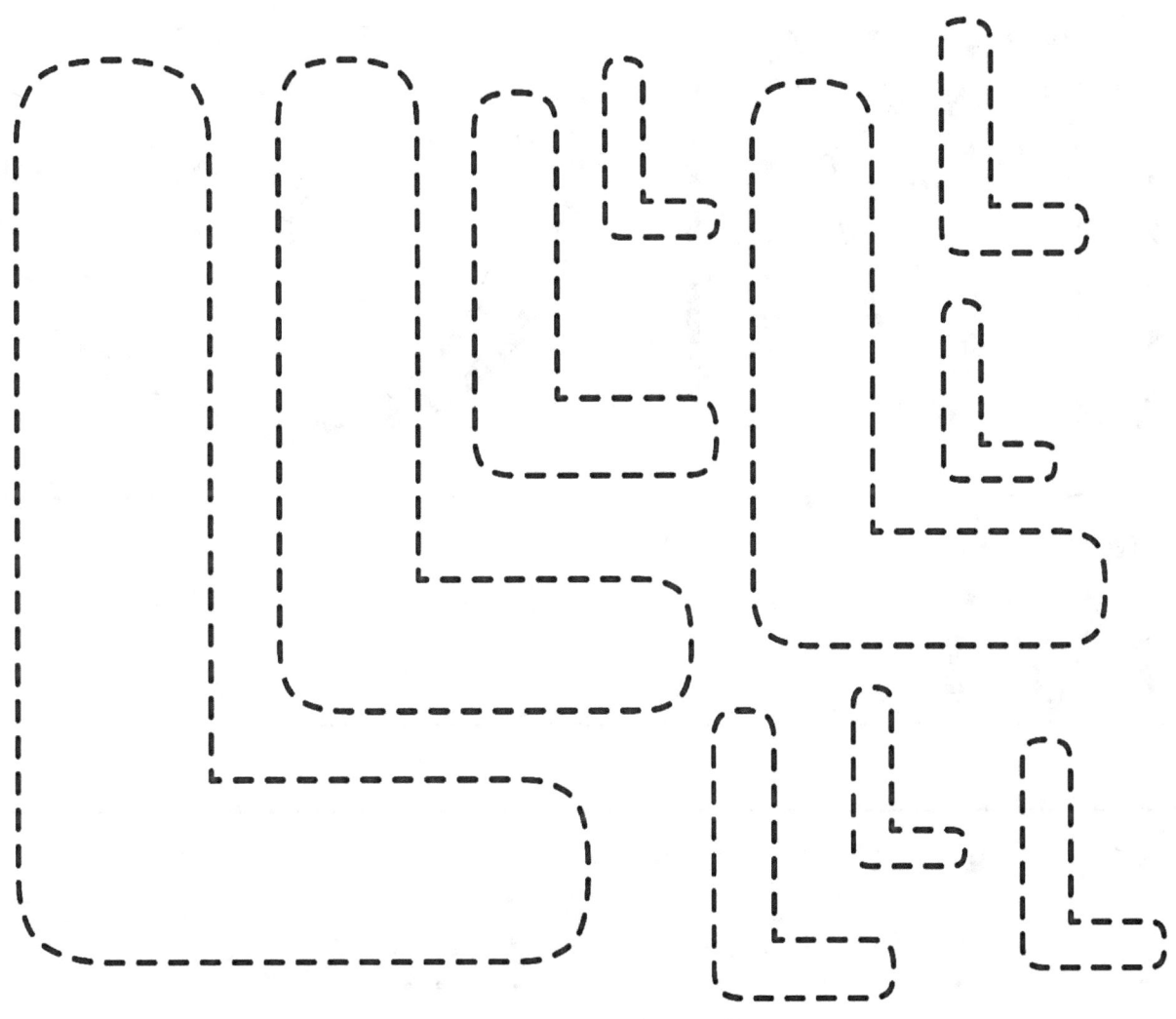

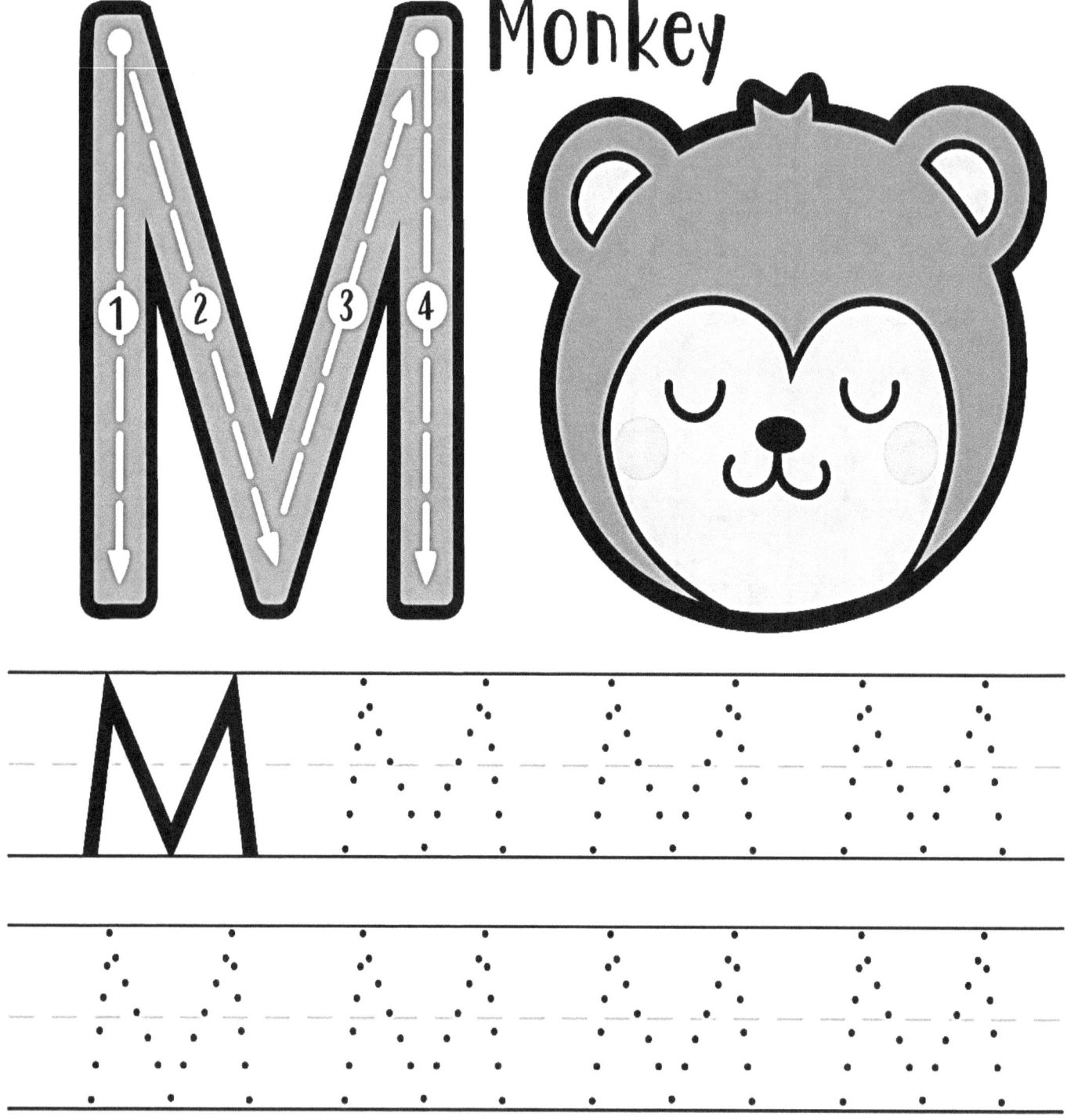

Trace & Color Letters

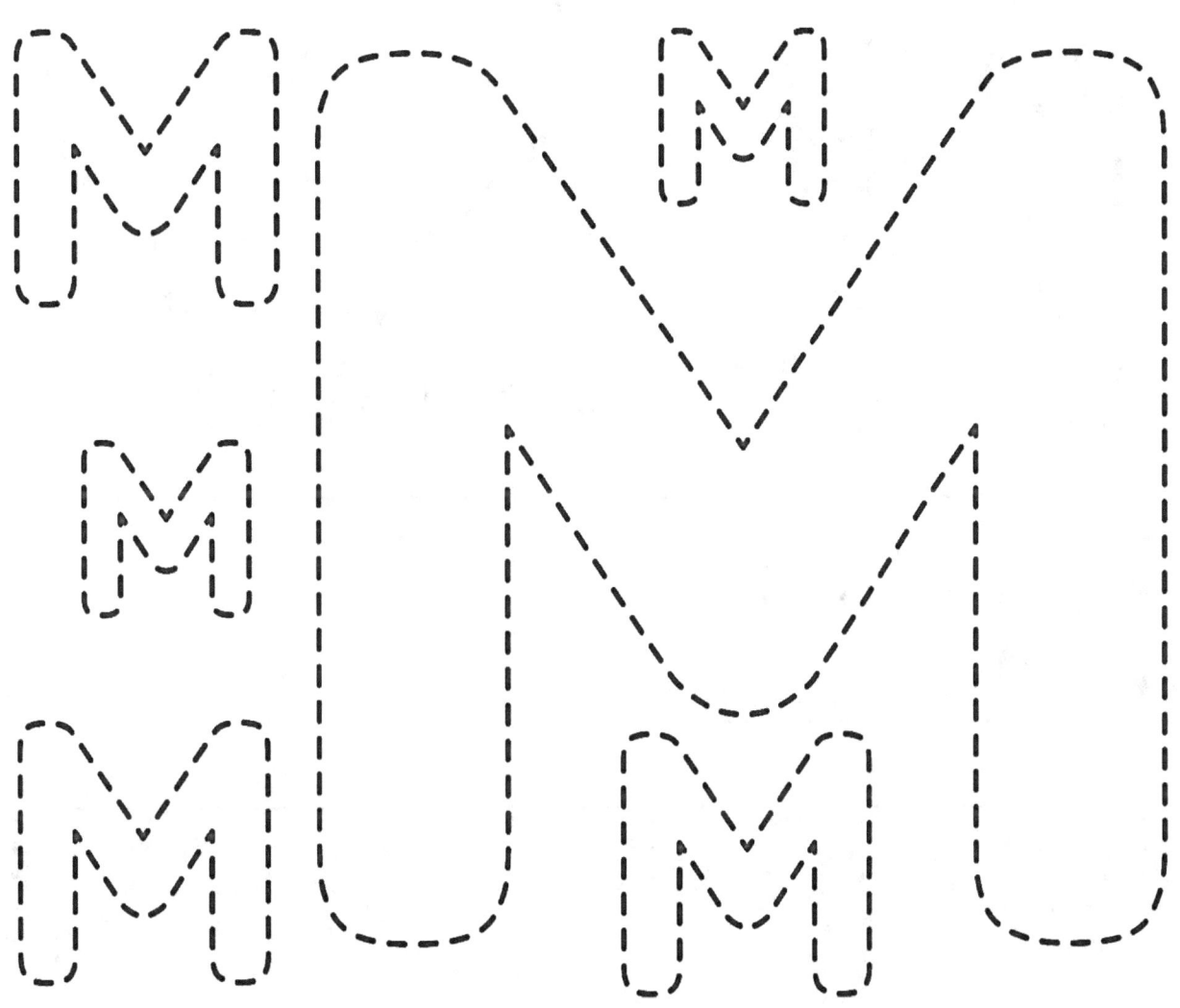

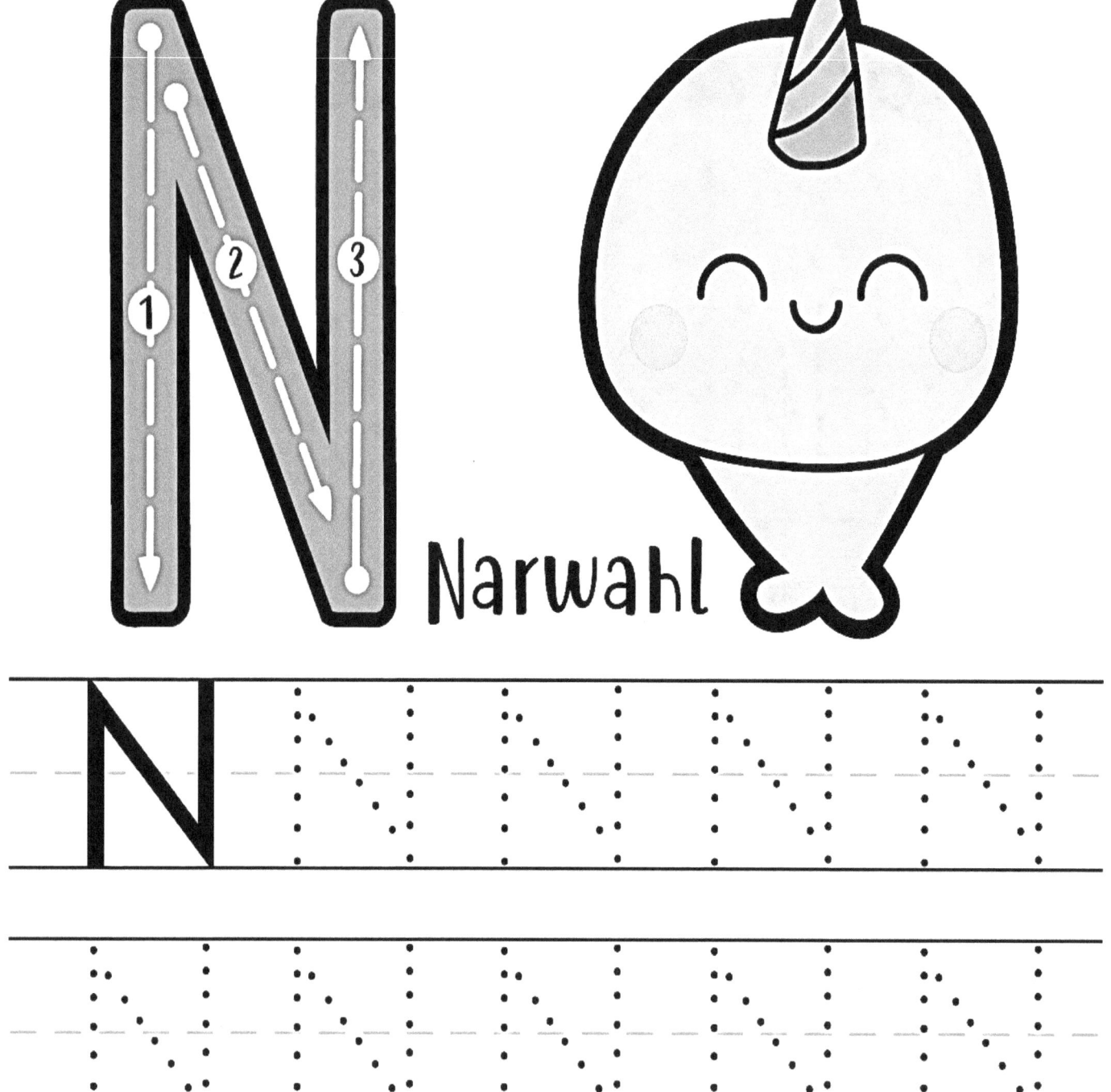

Narwahl

Trace & Color Letters

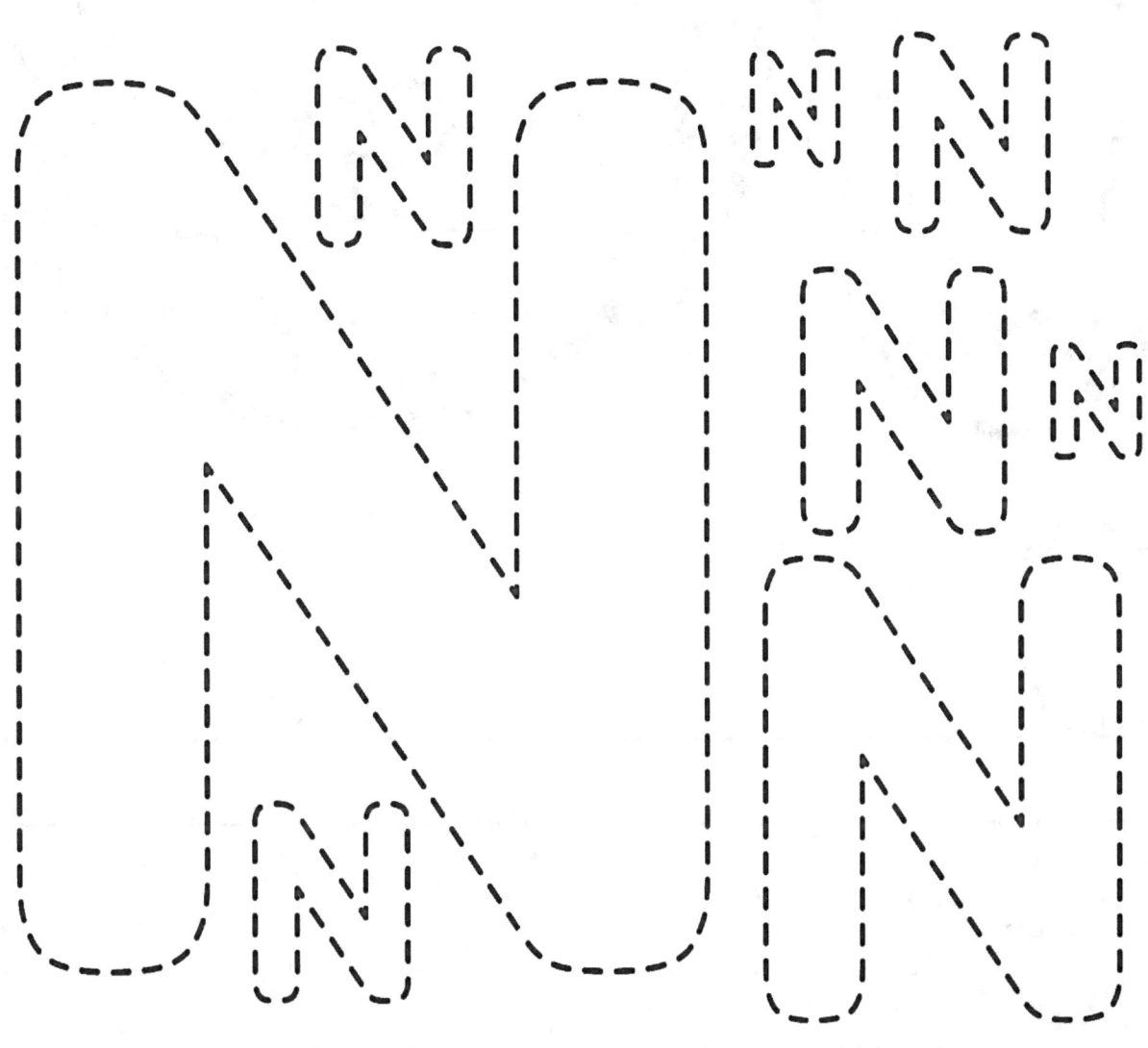

Owl

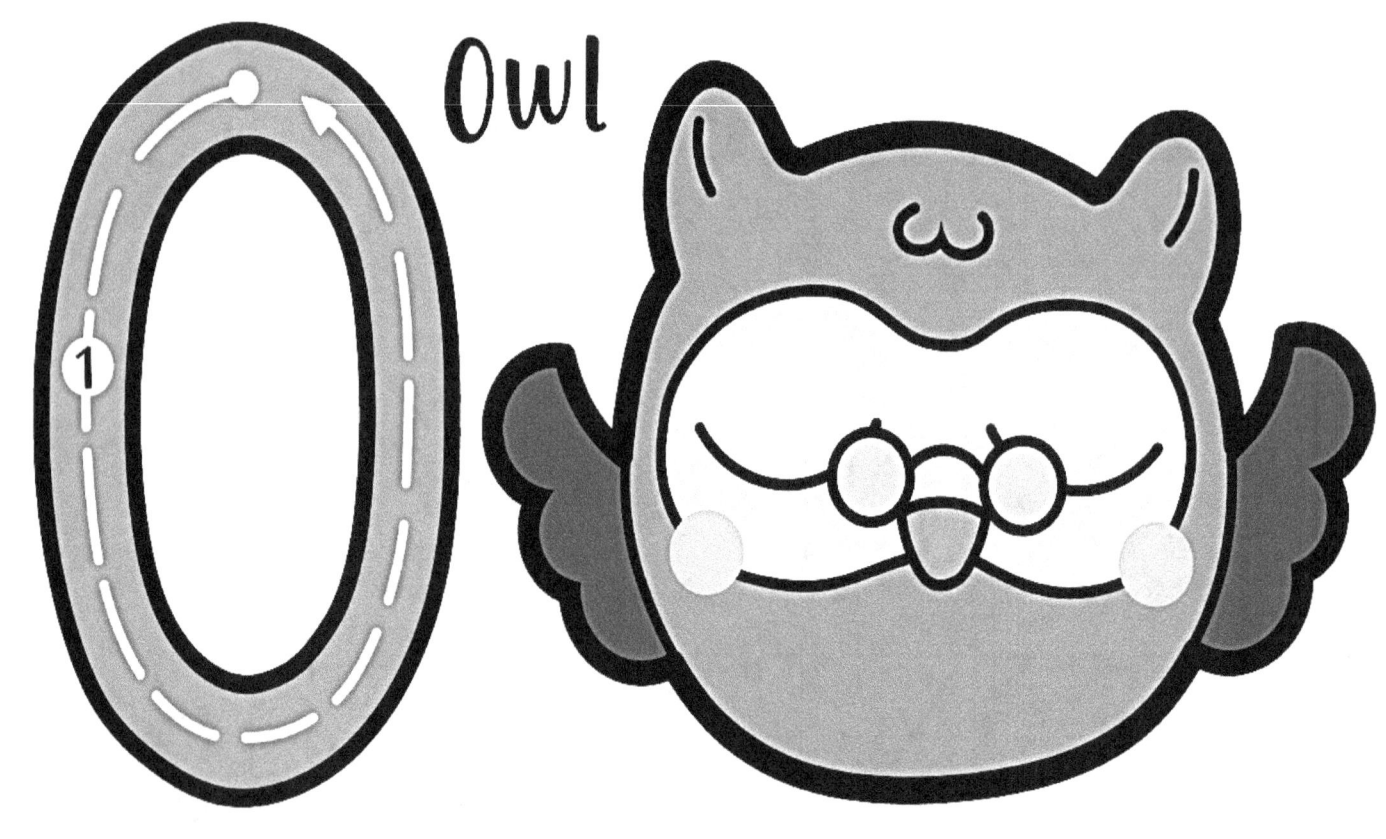

Trace & Color Letters

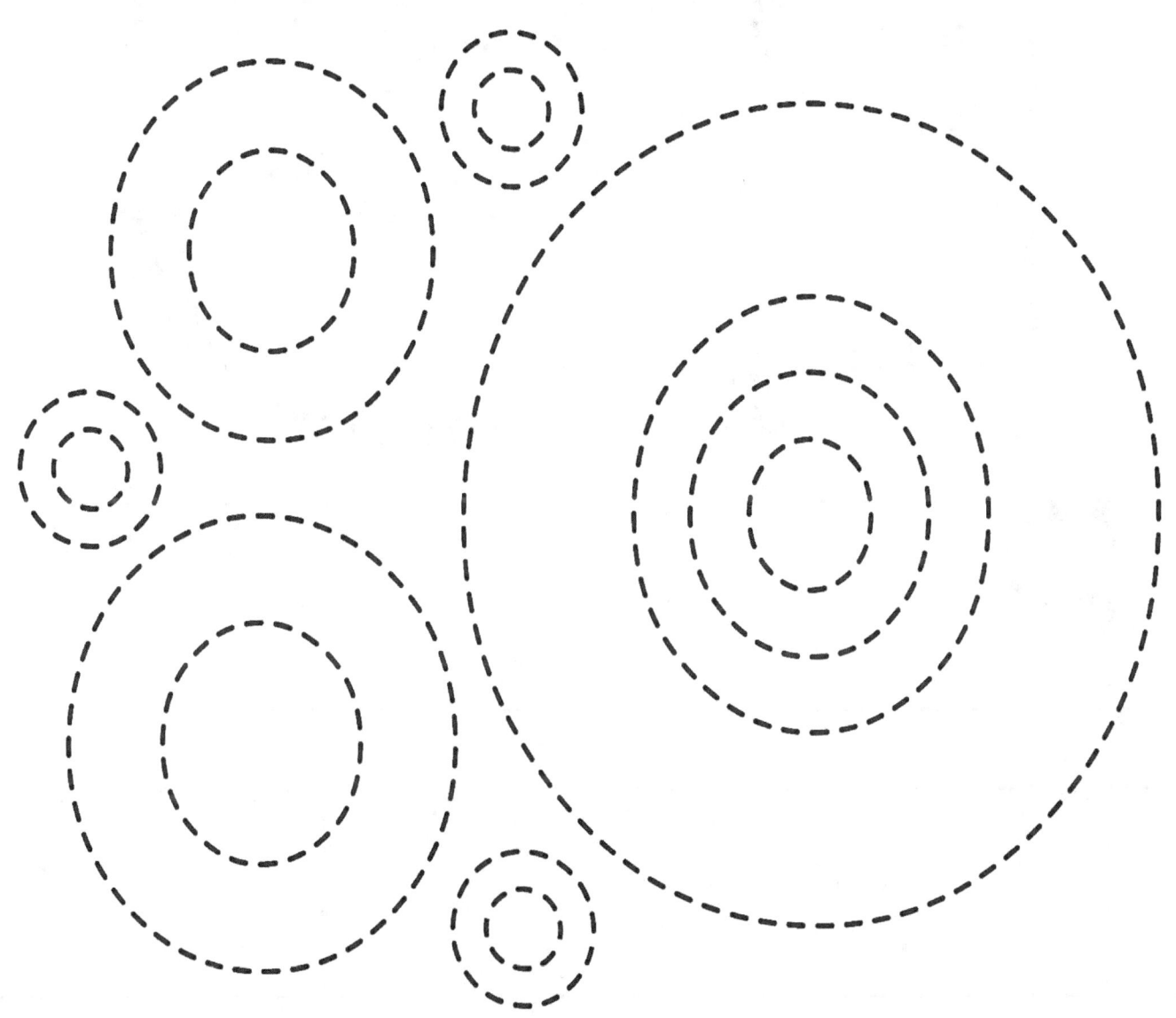

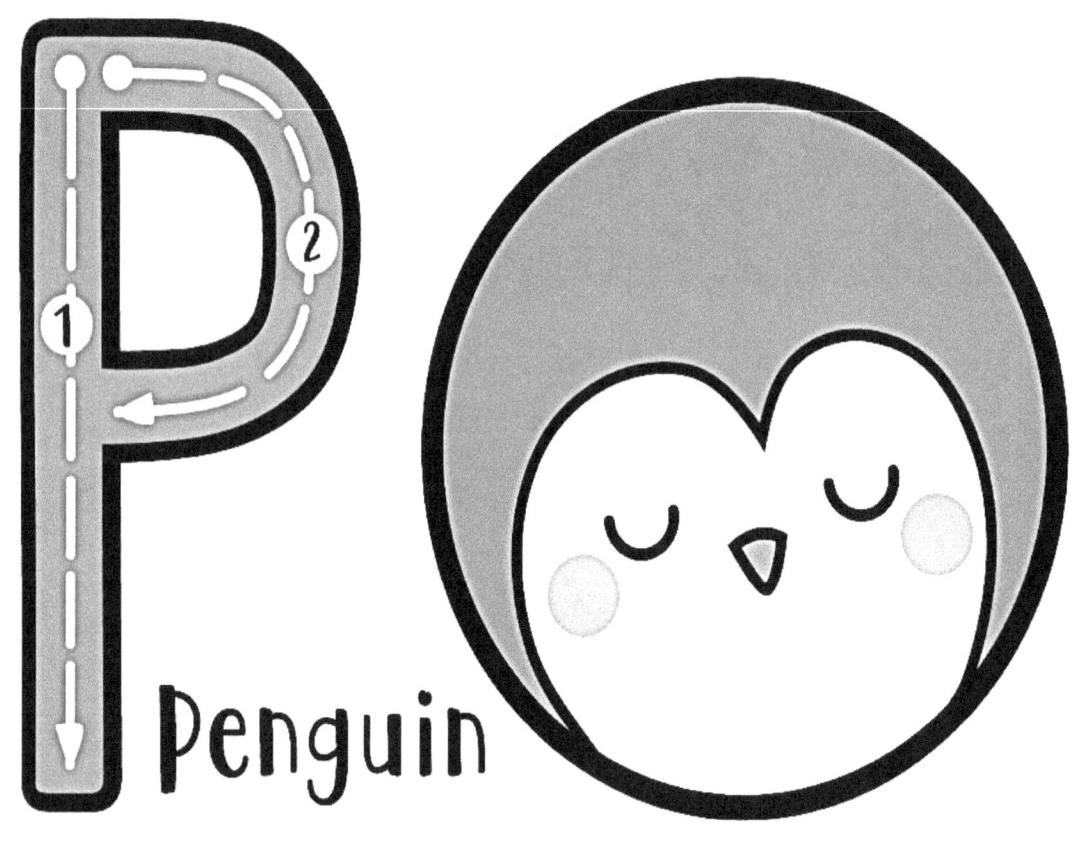

Penguin

Trace & Color Letters

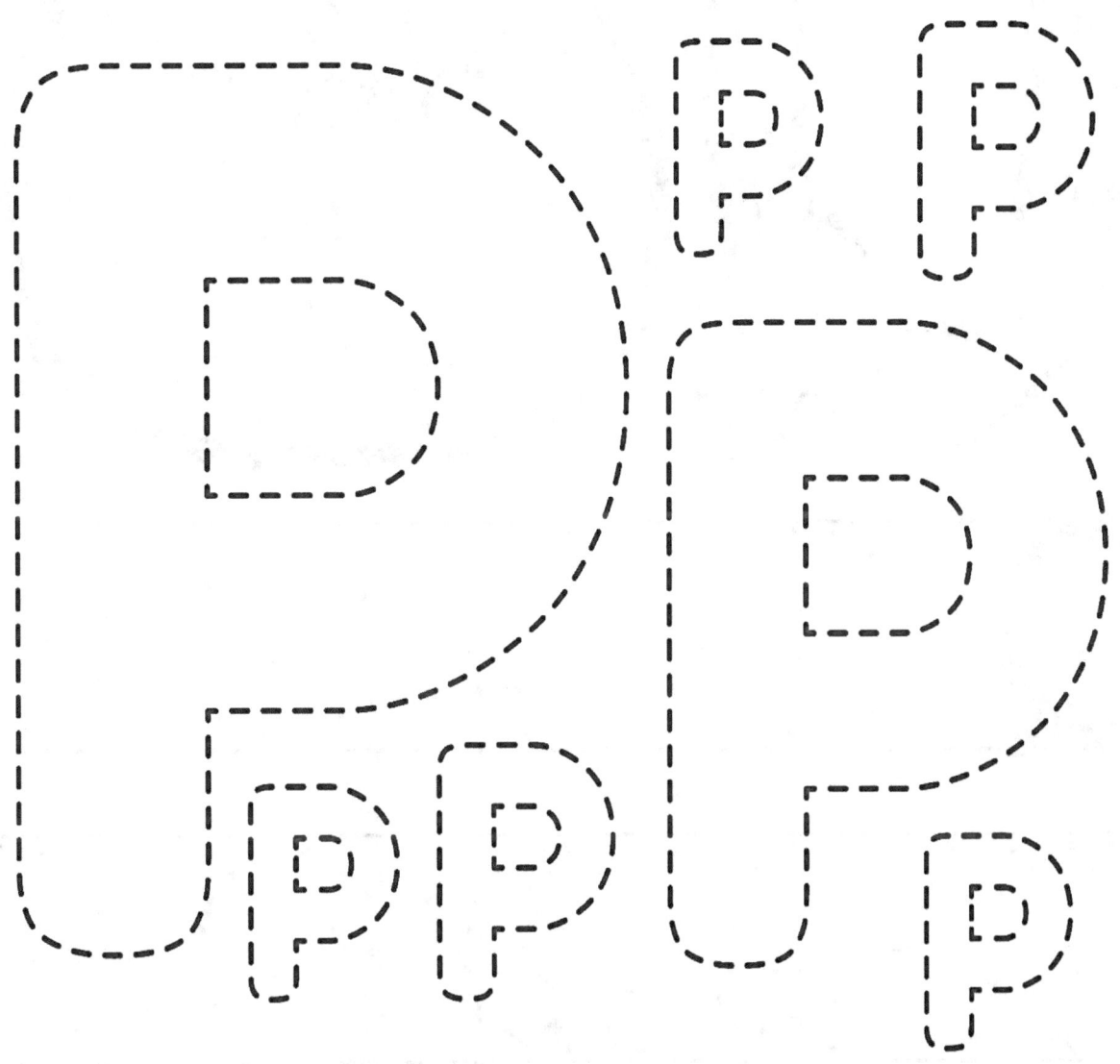

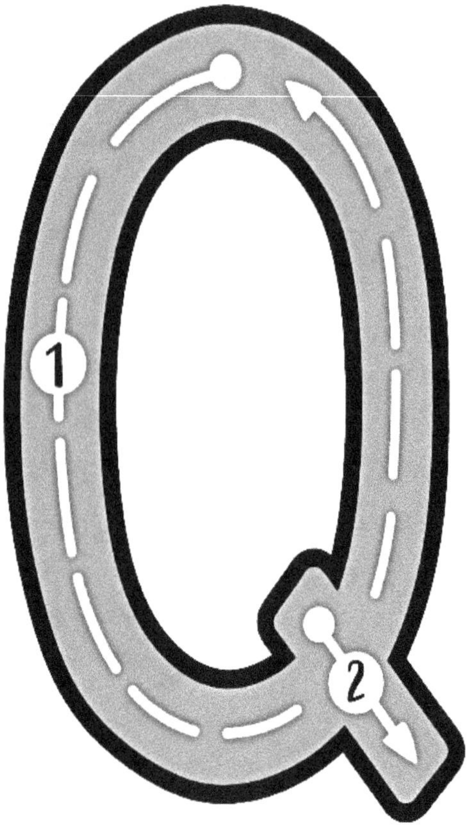

Quokka

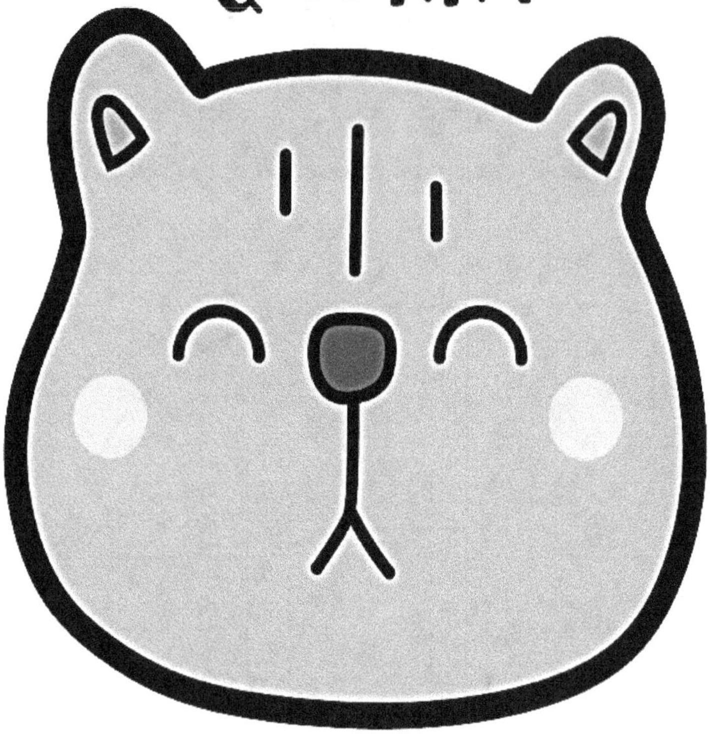

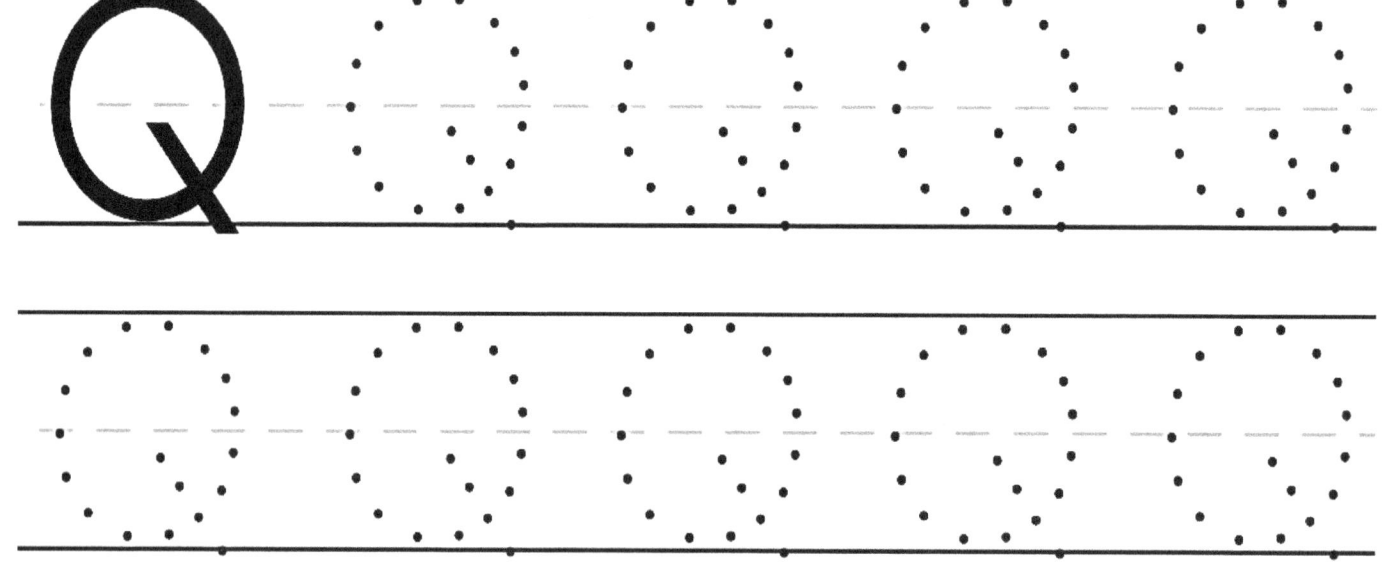

Trace & Color Letters

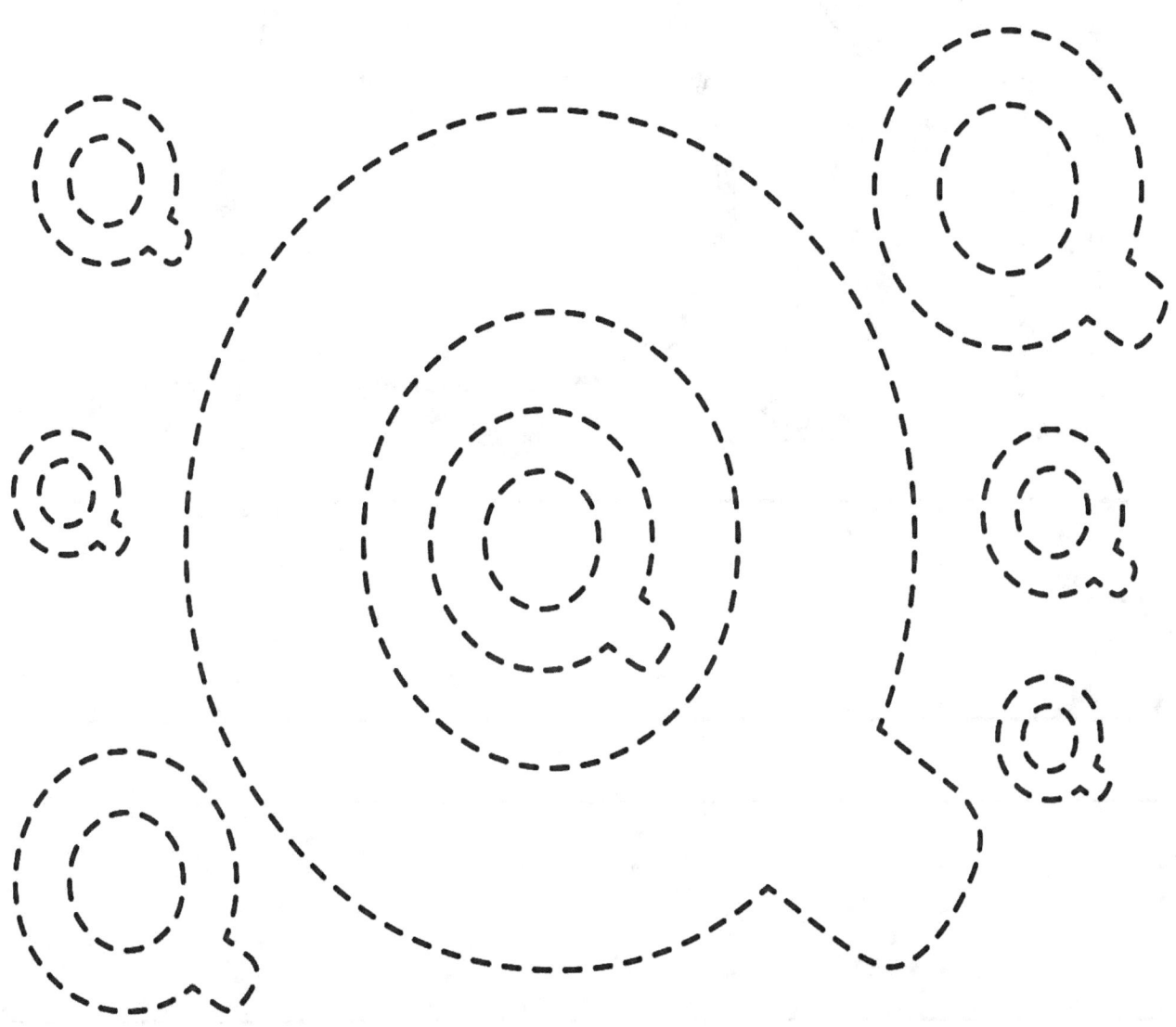

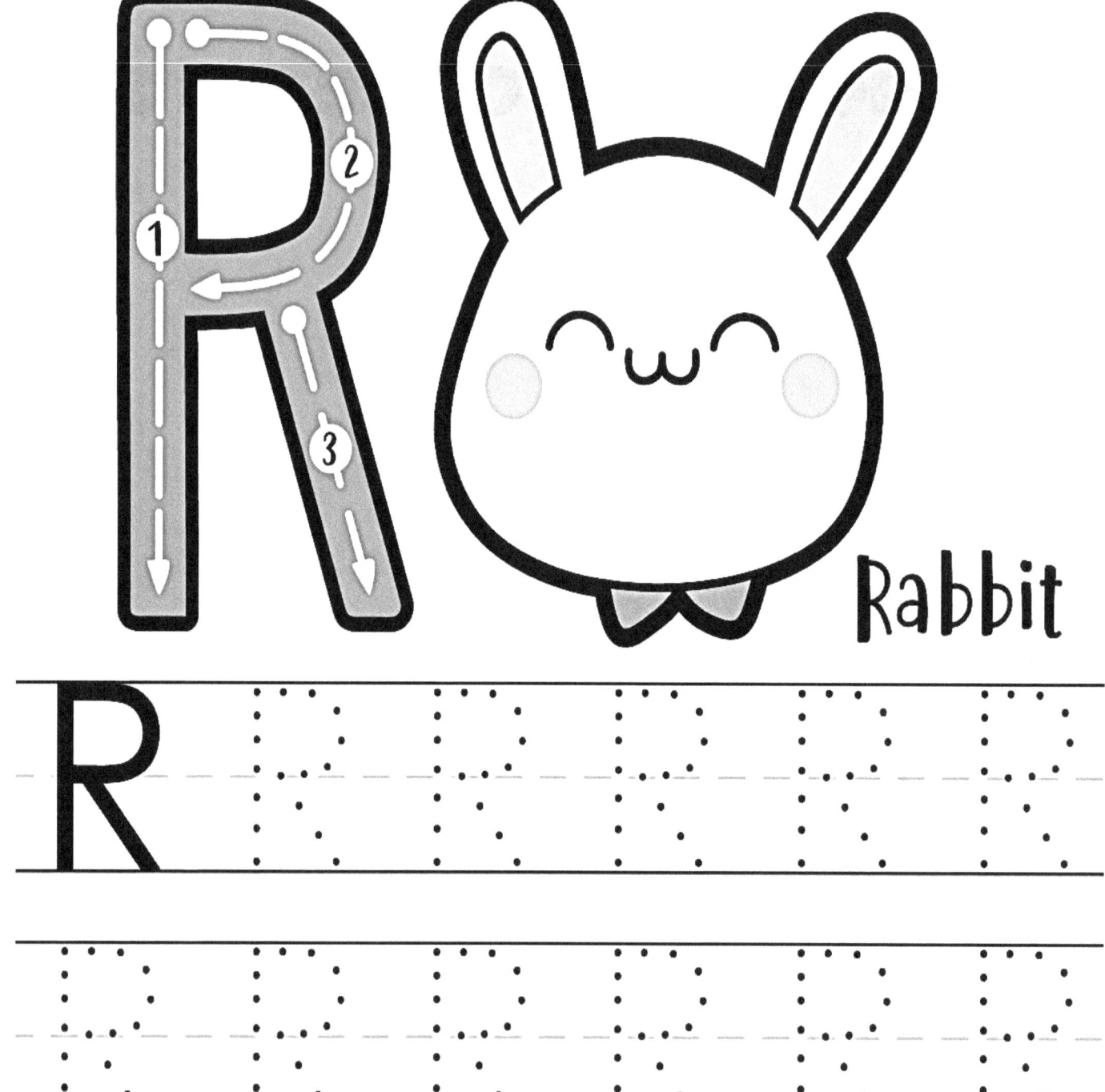

Trace & Color Letters

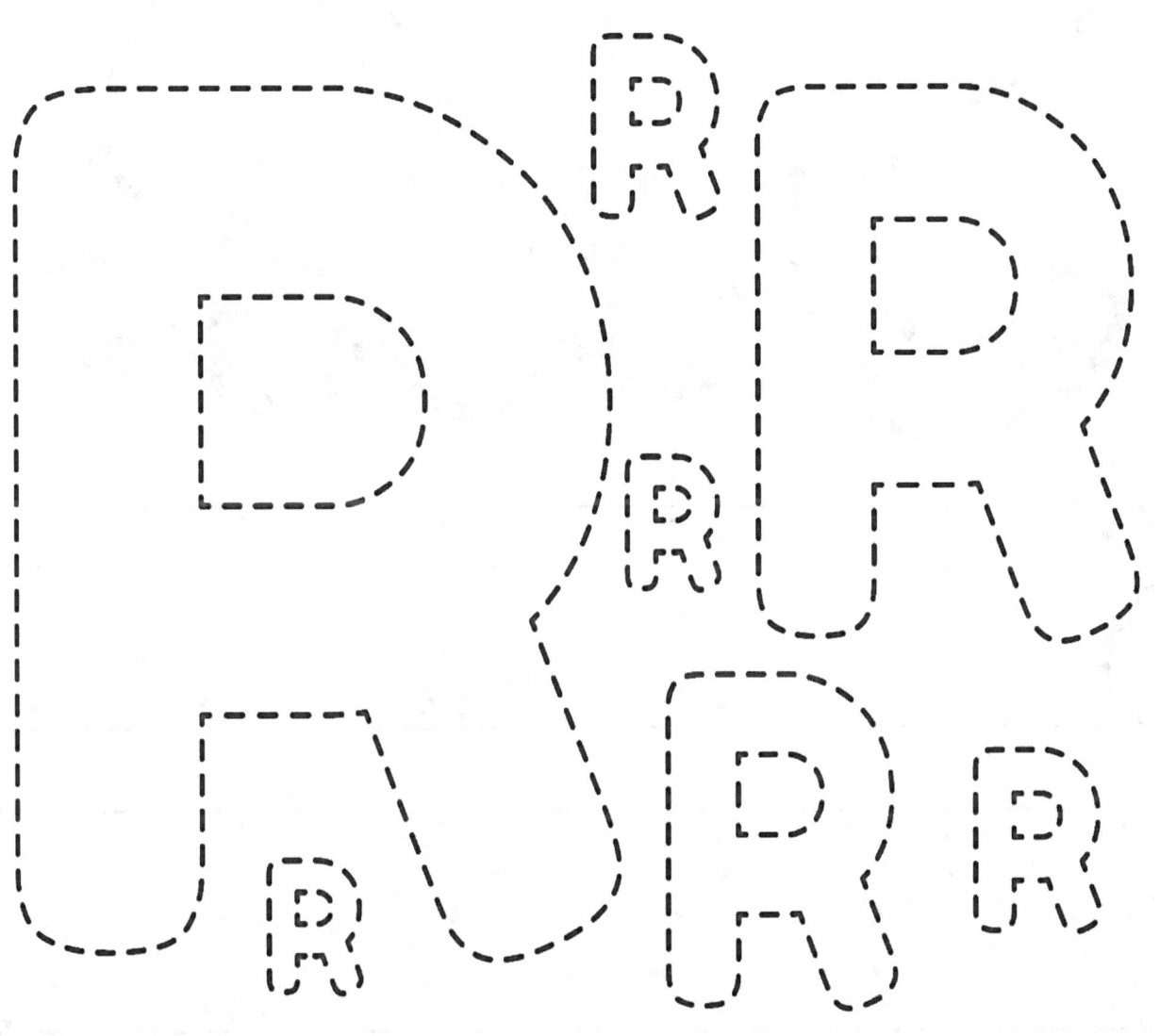

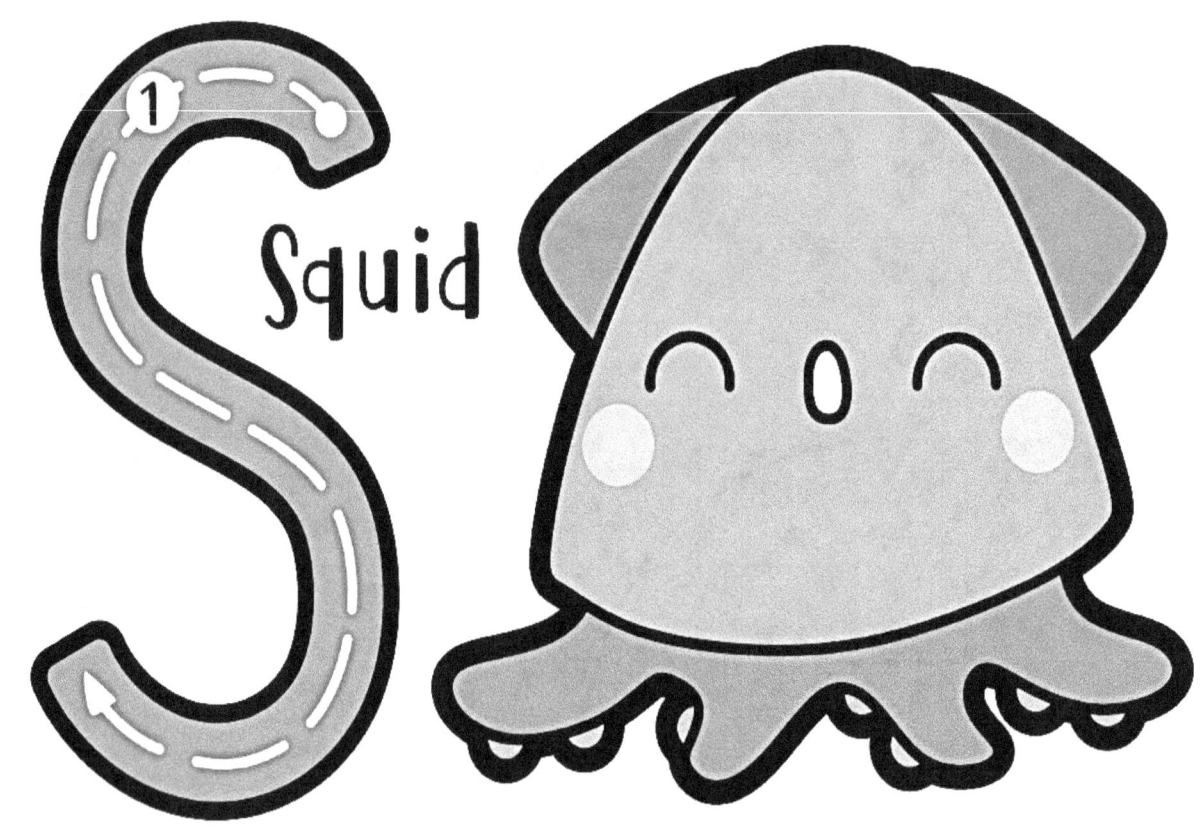

Trace & Color Letters

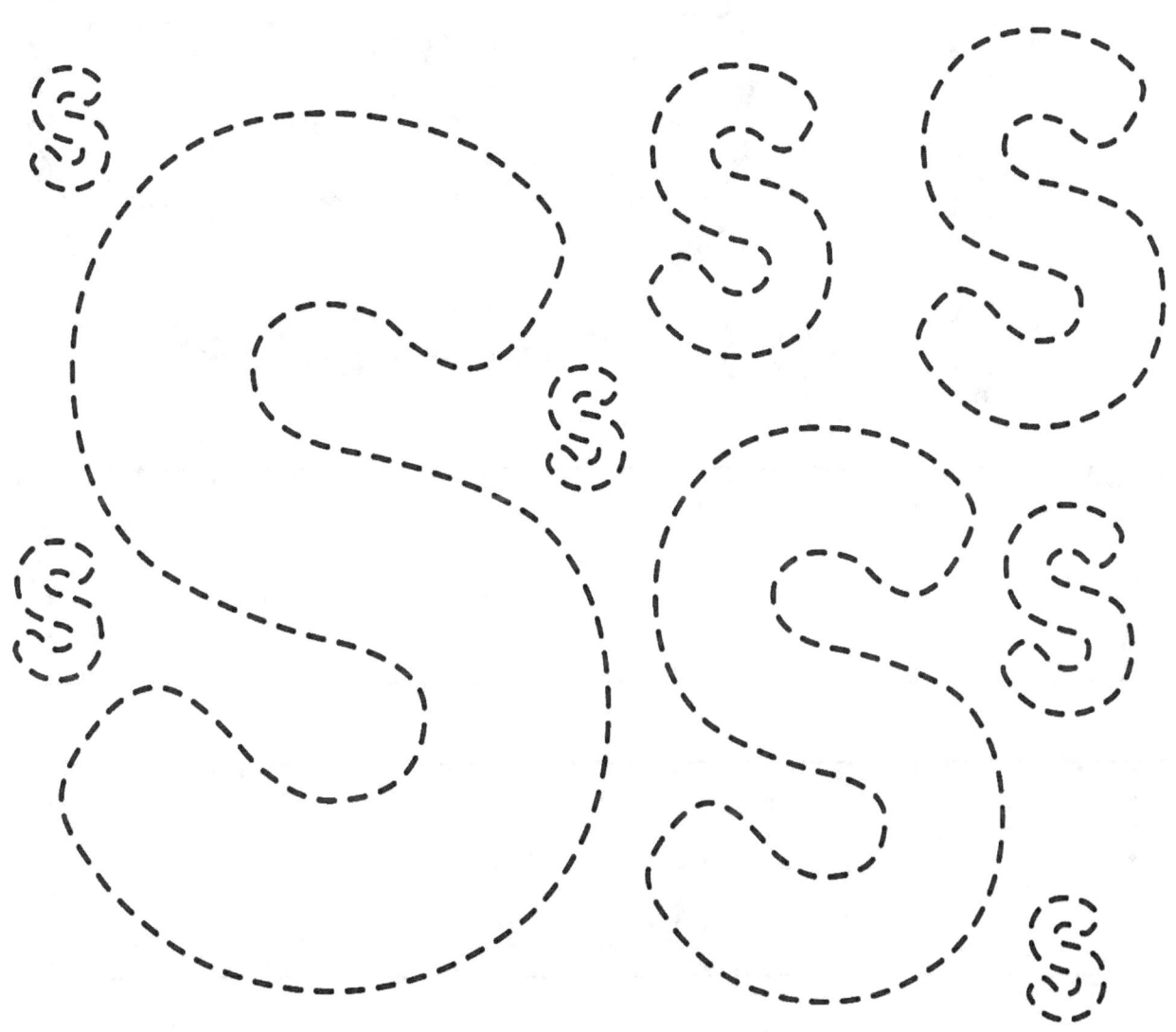

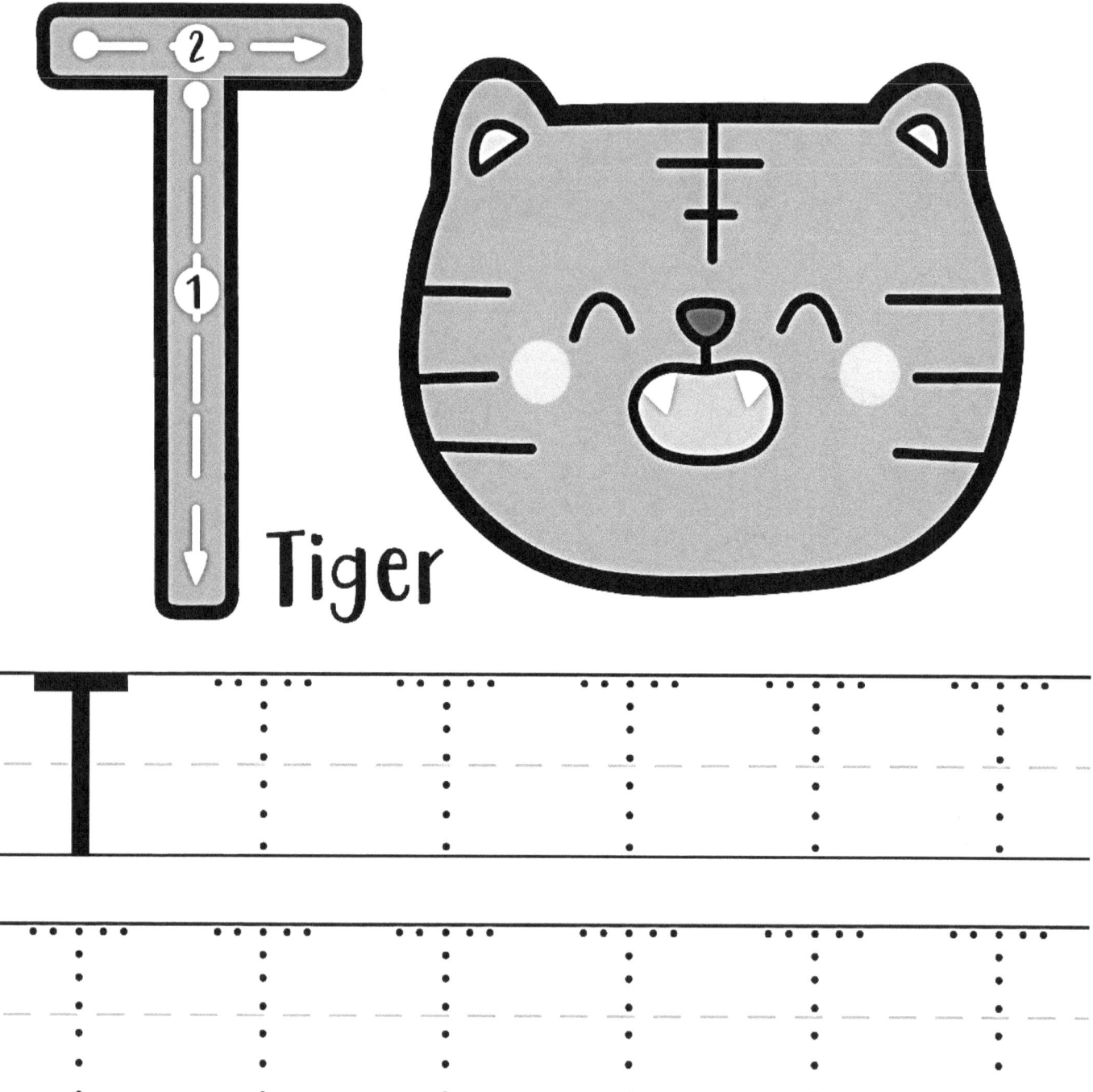
Tiger

Trace & Color Letters

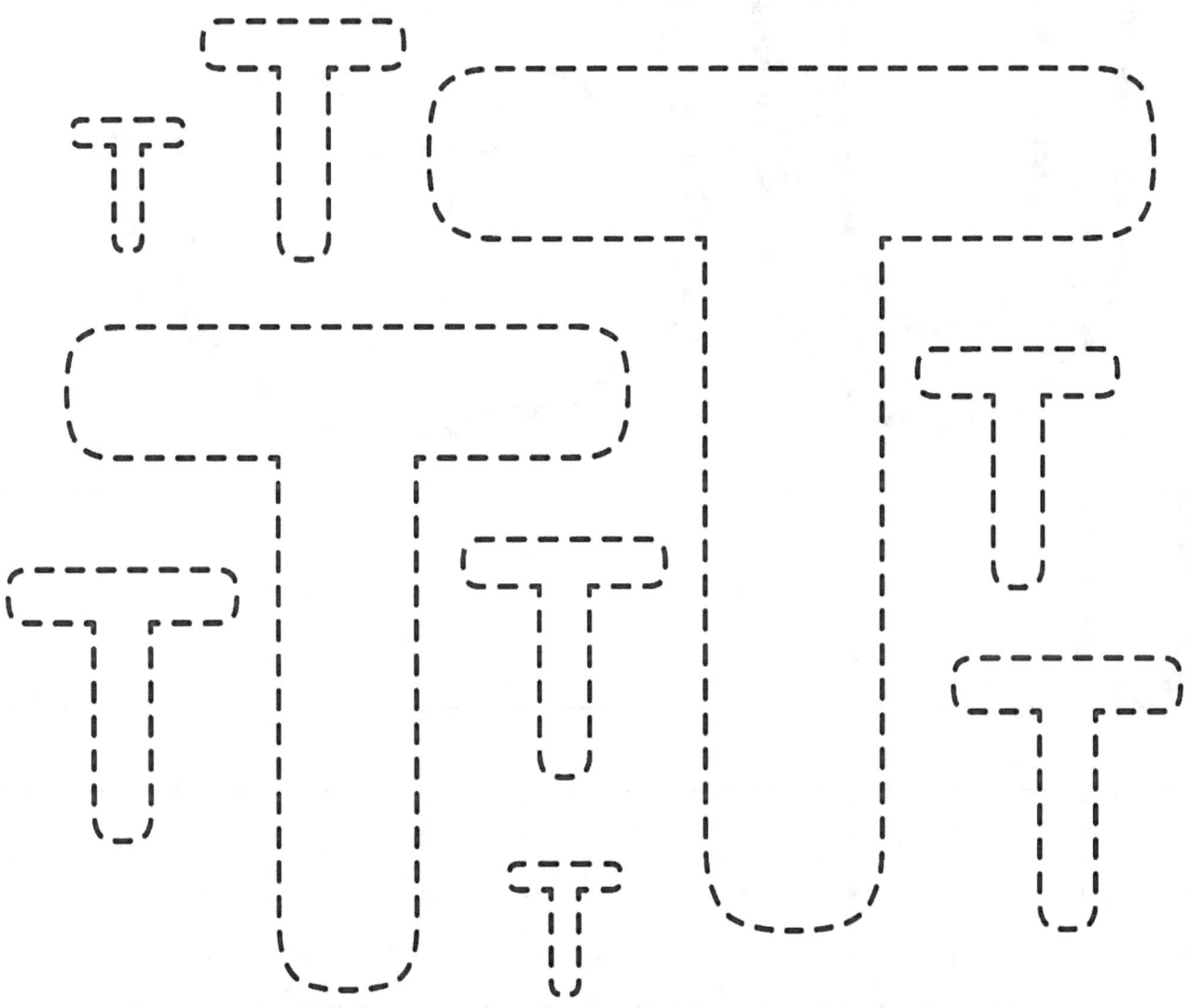

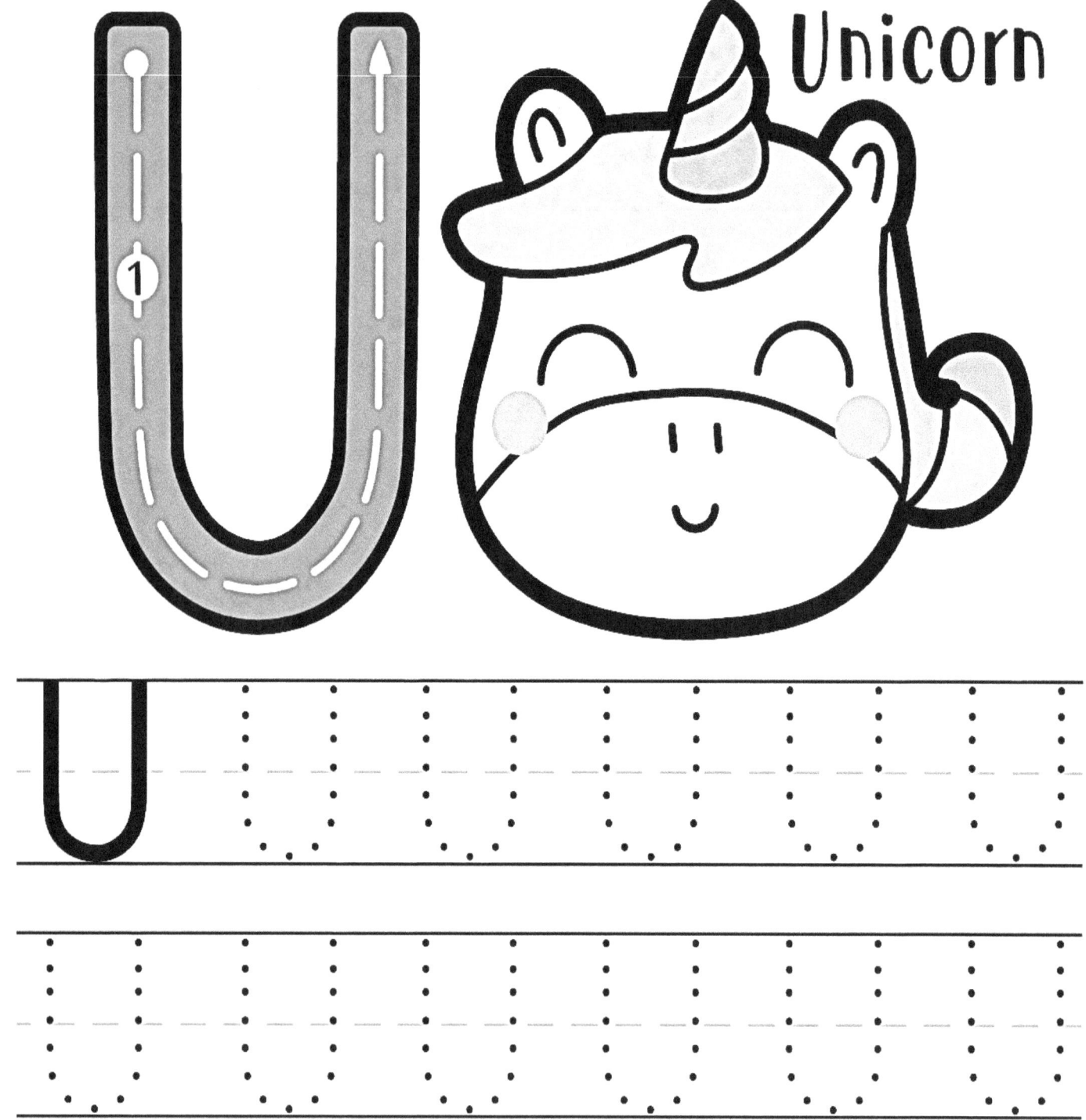

Trace & Color Letters

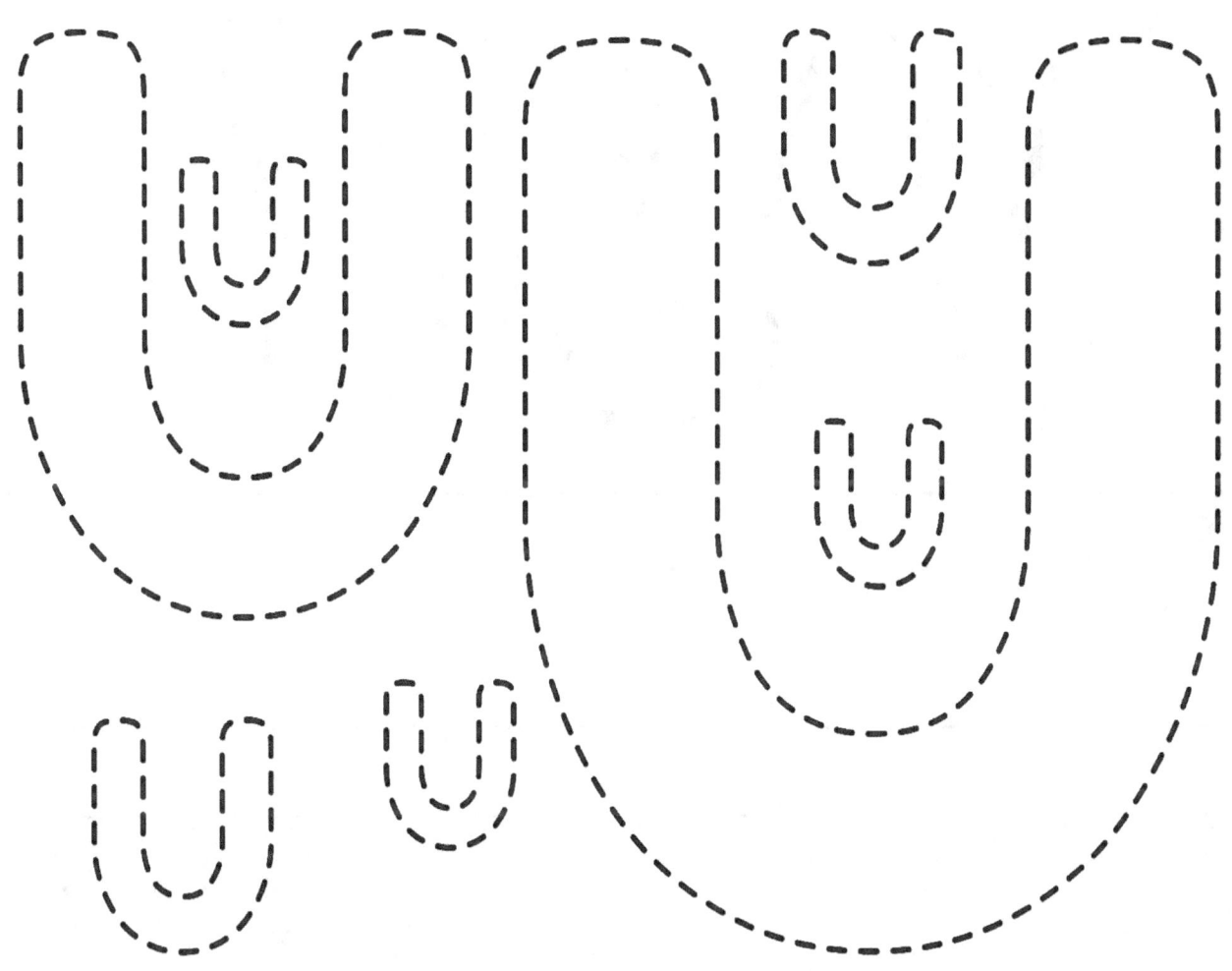

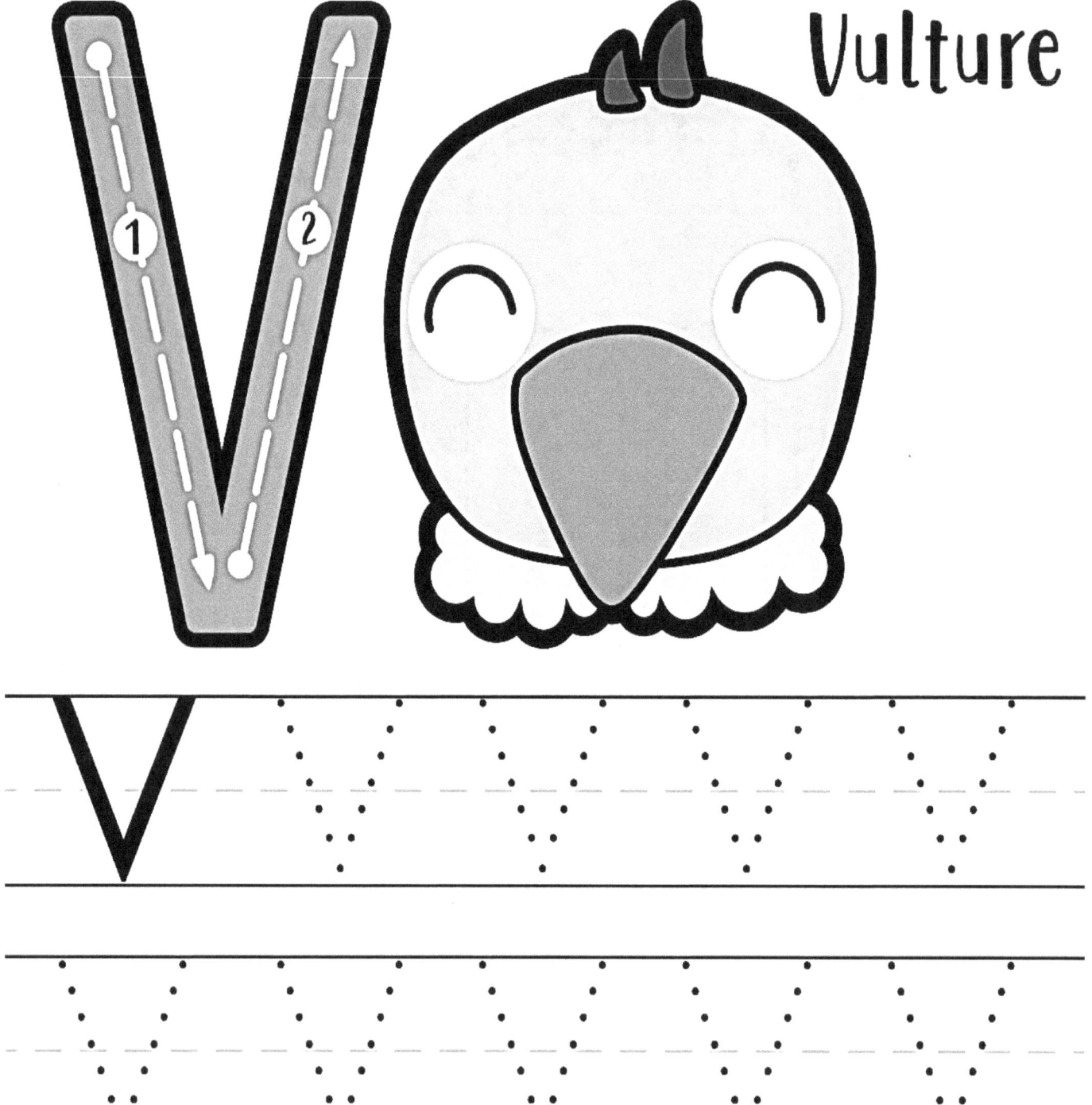

Vulture

Trace & Color Letters

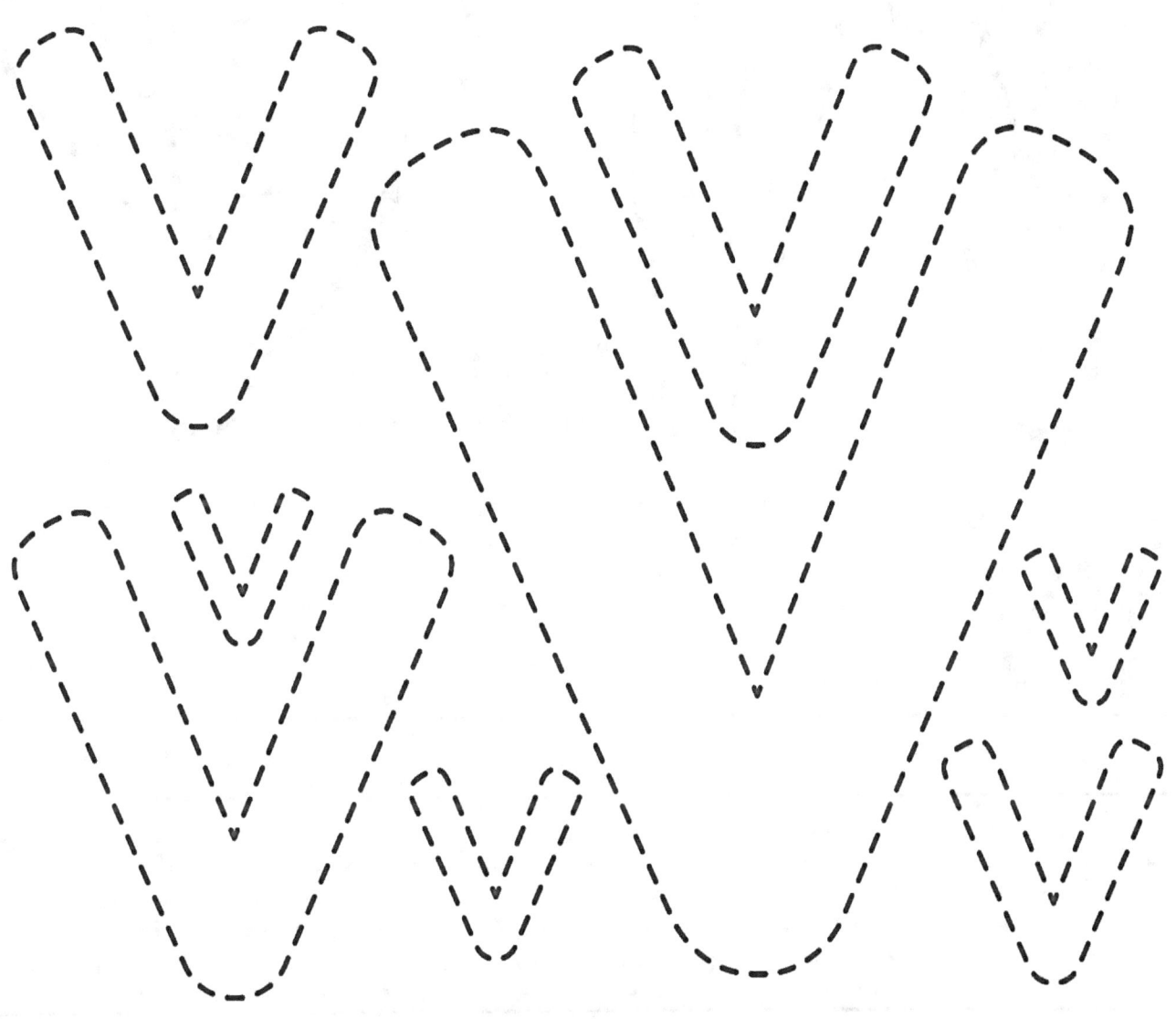

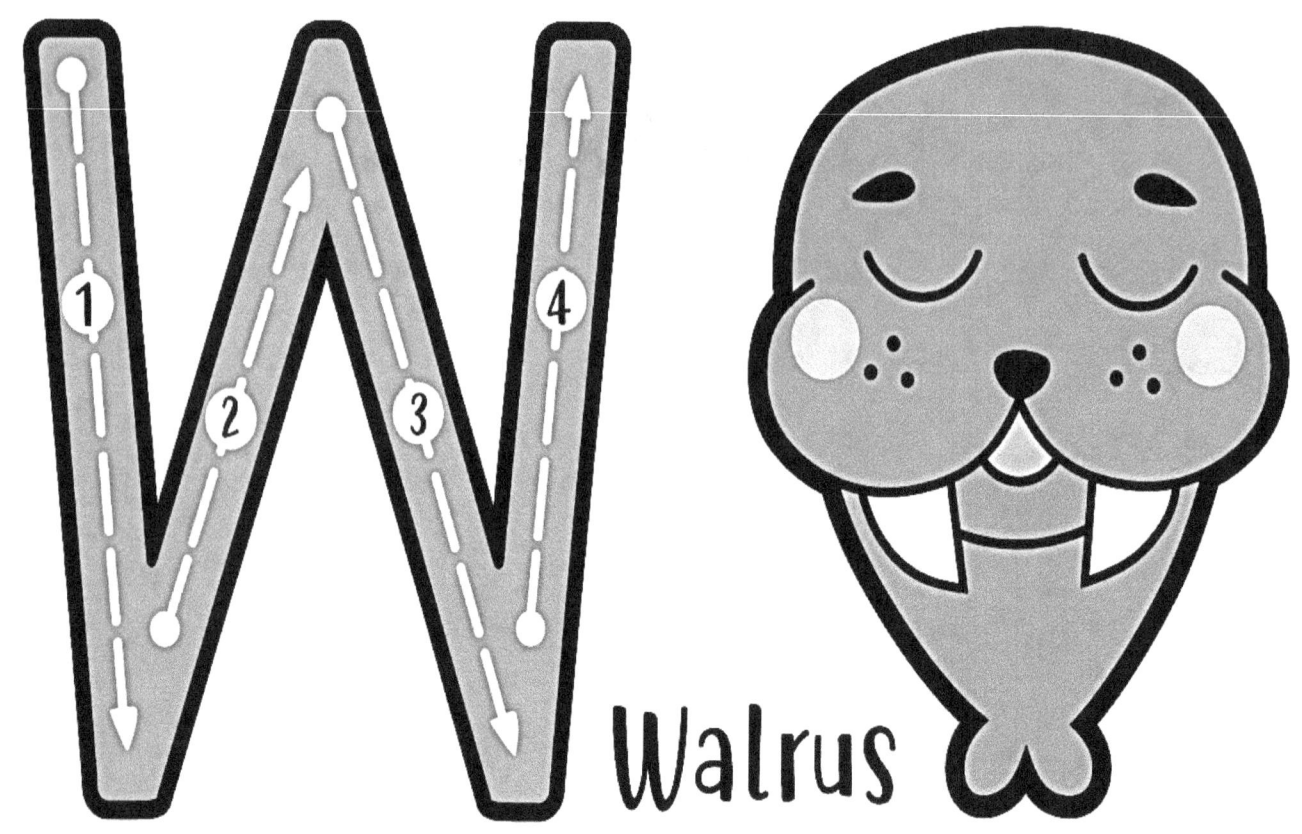

Walrus

Trace & Color Letters

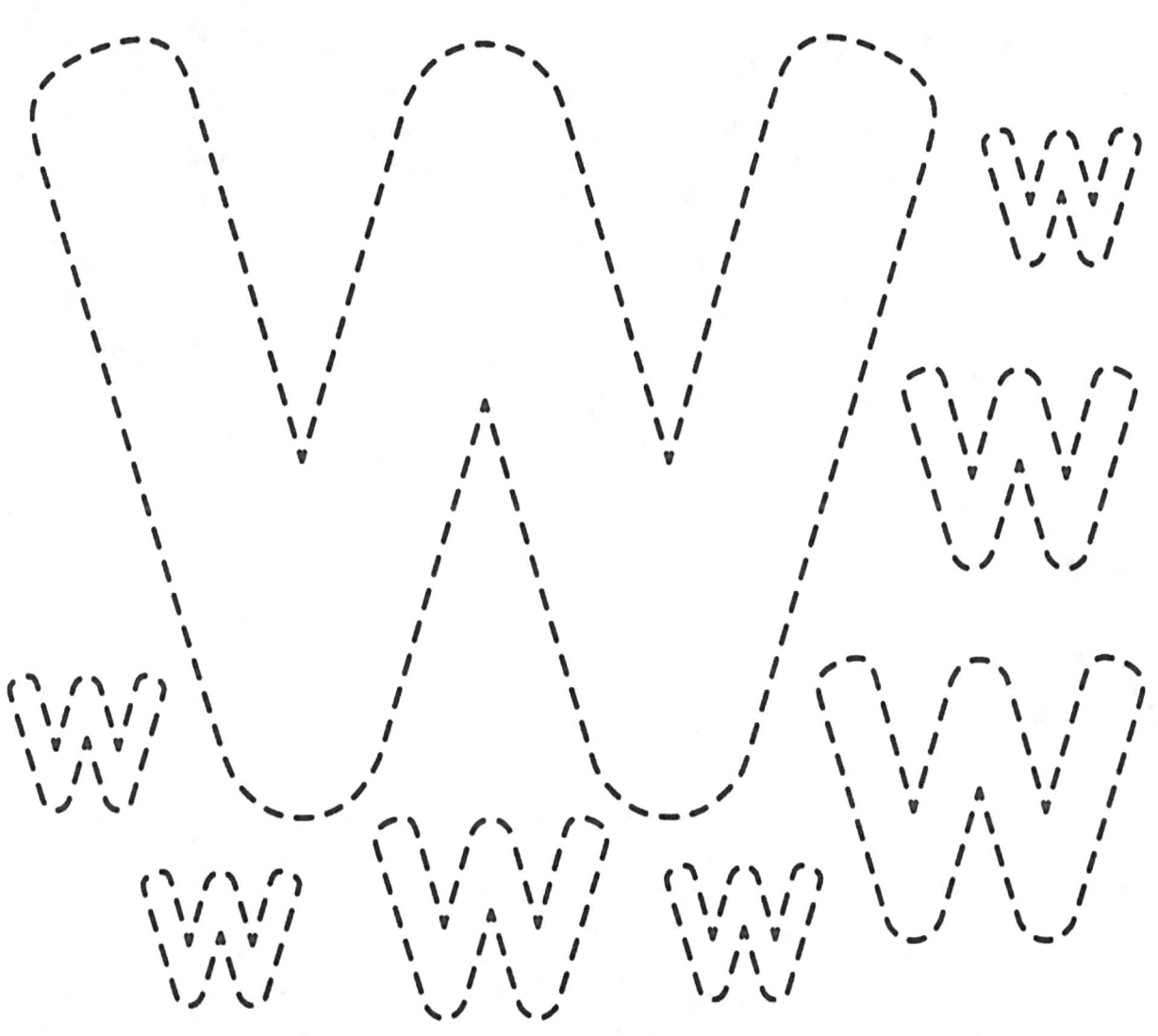

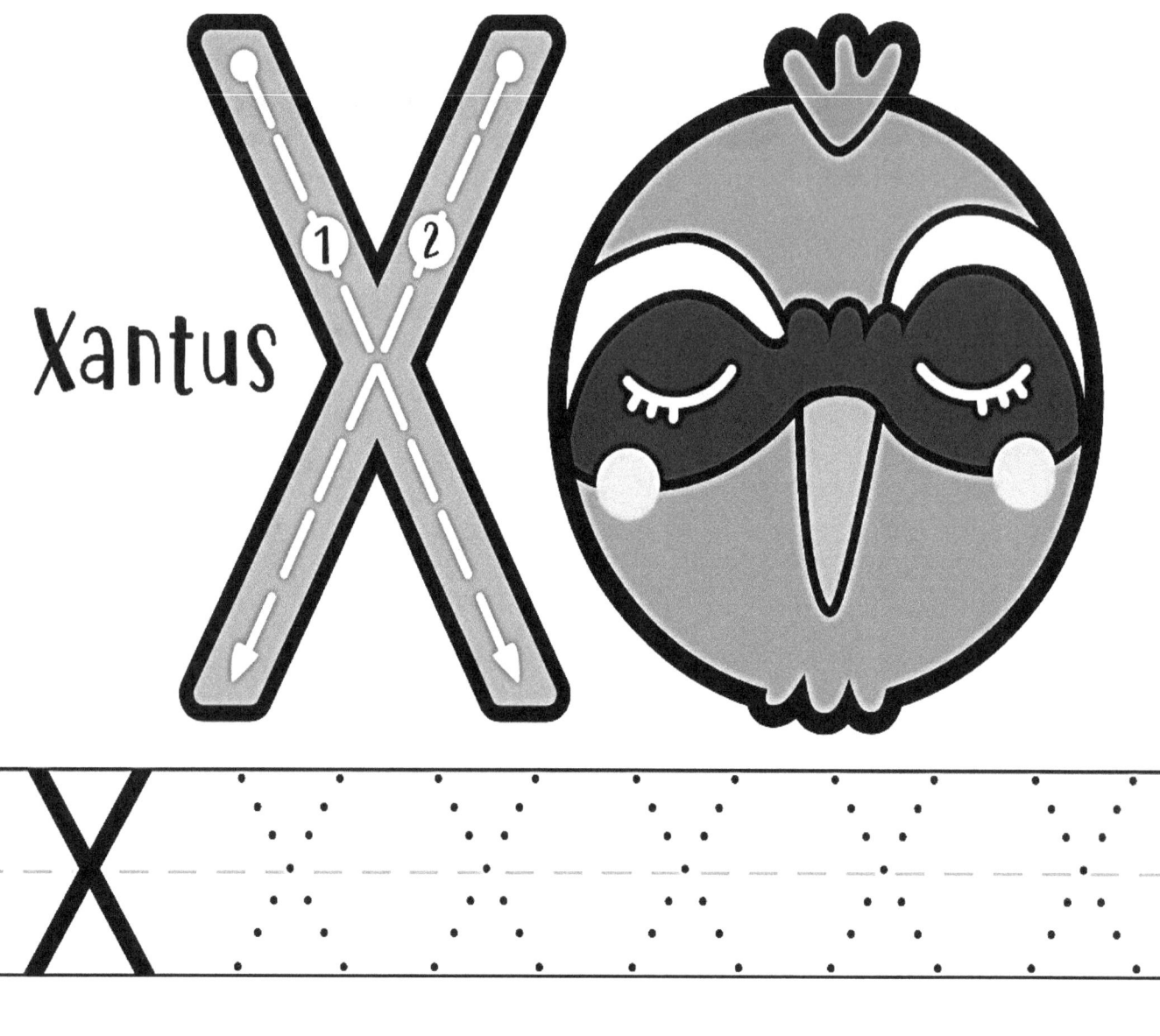

Xantus

Trace & Color Letters

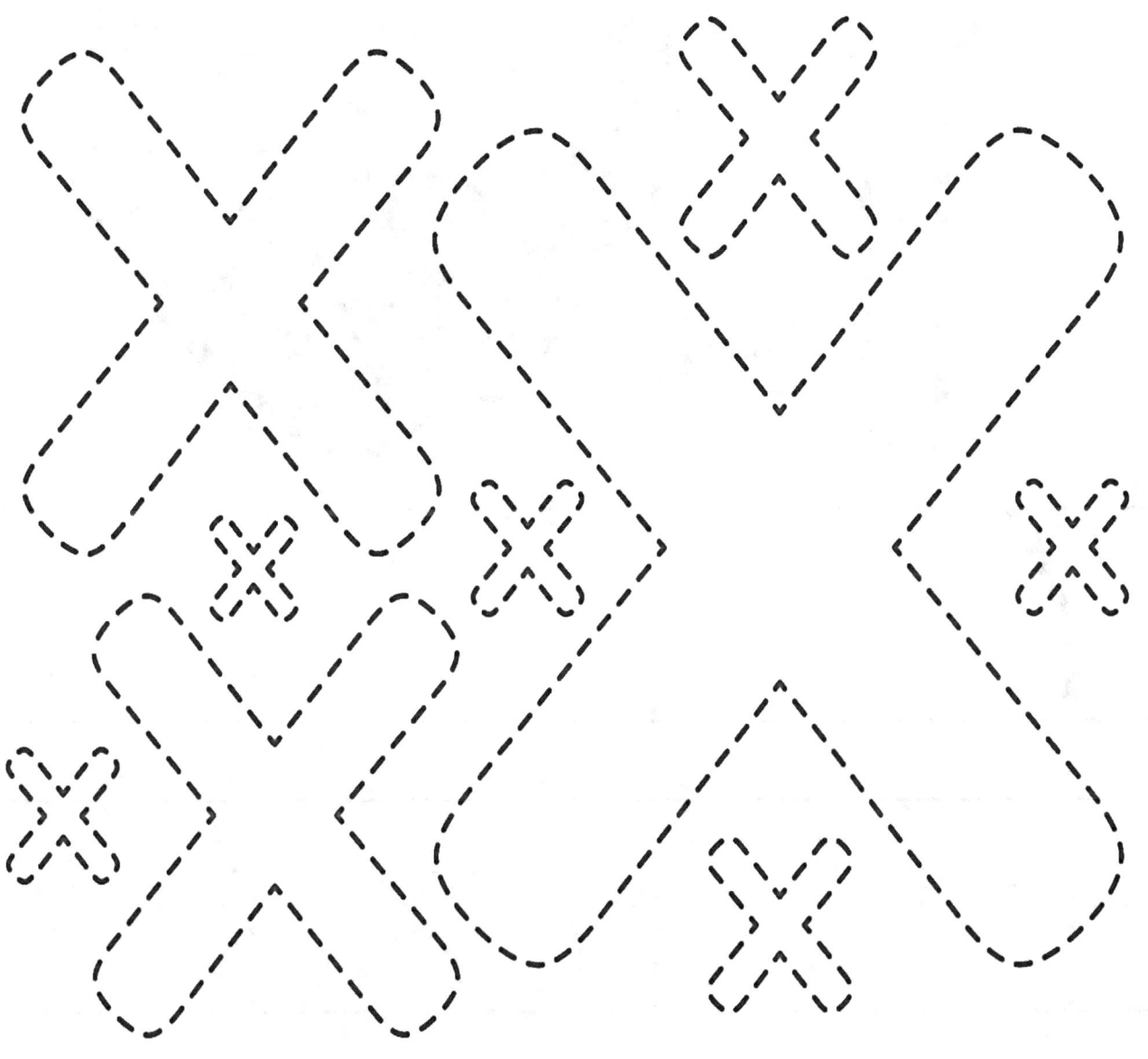

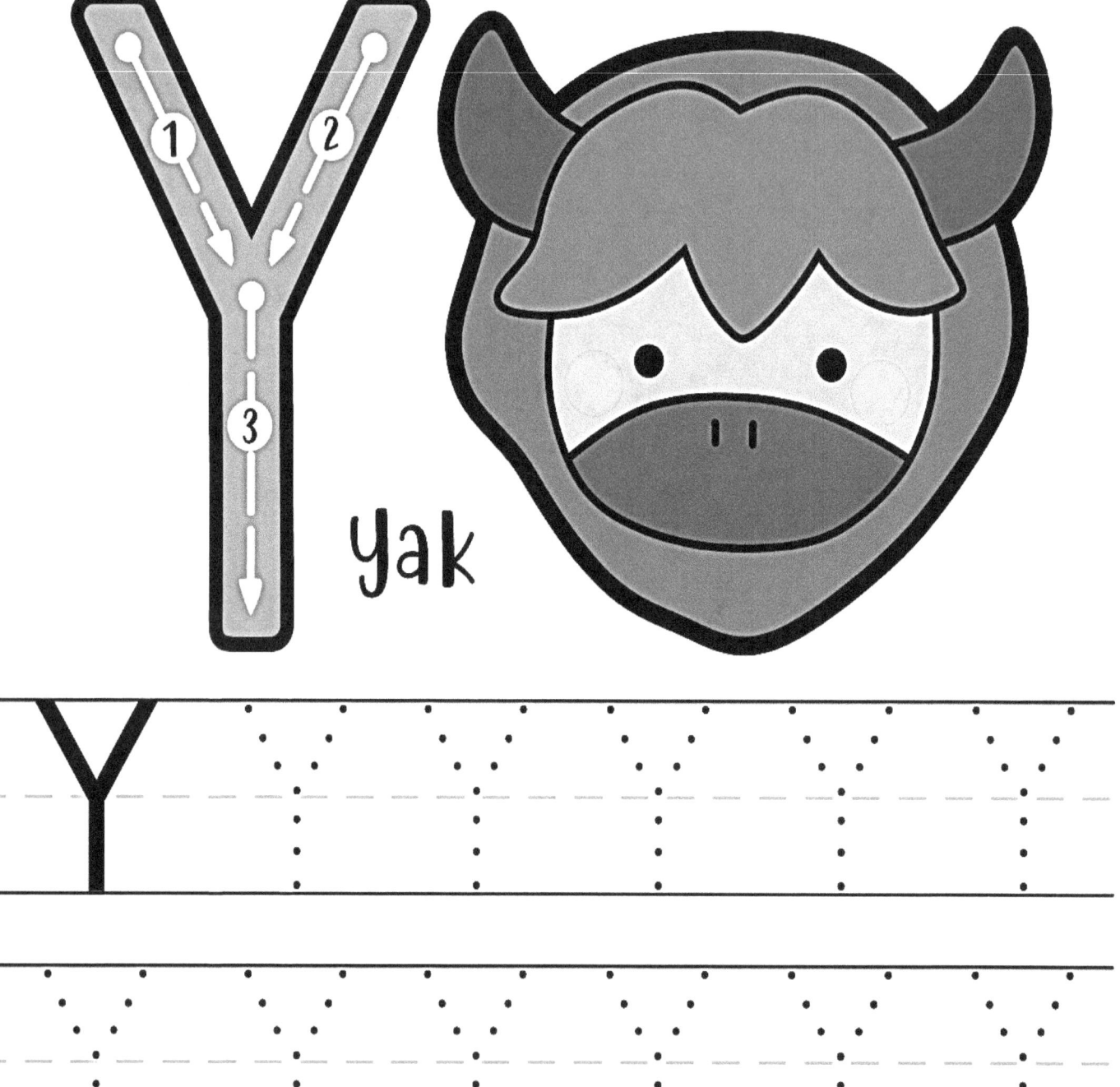

yak

Trace & Color Letters

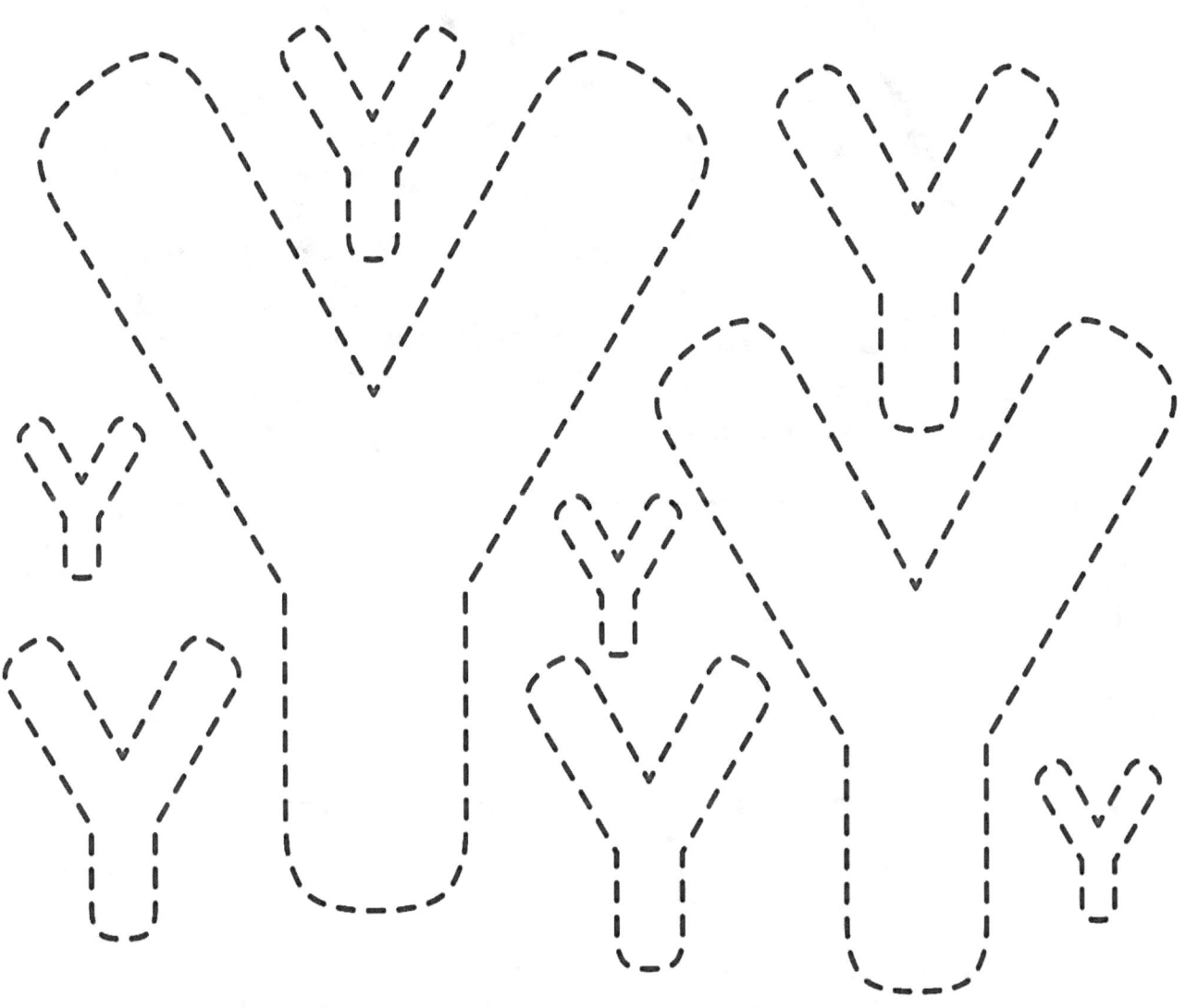

zebra

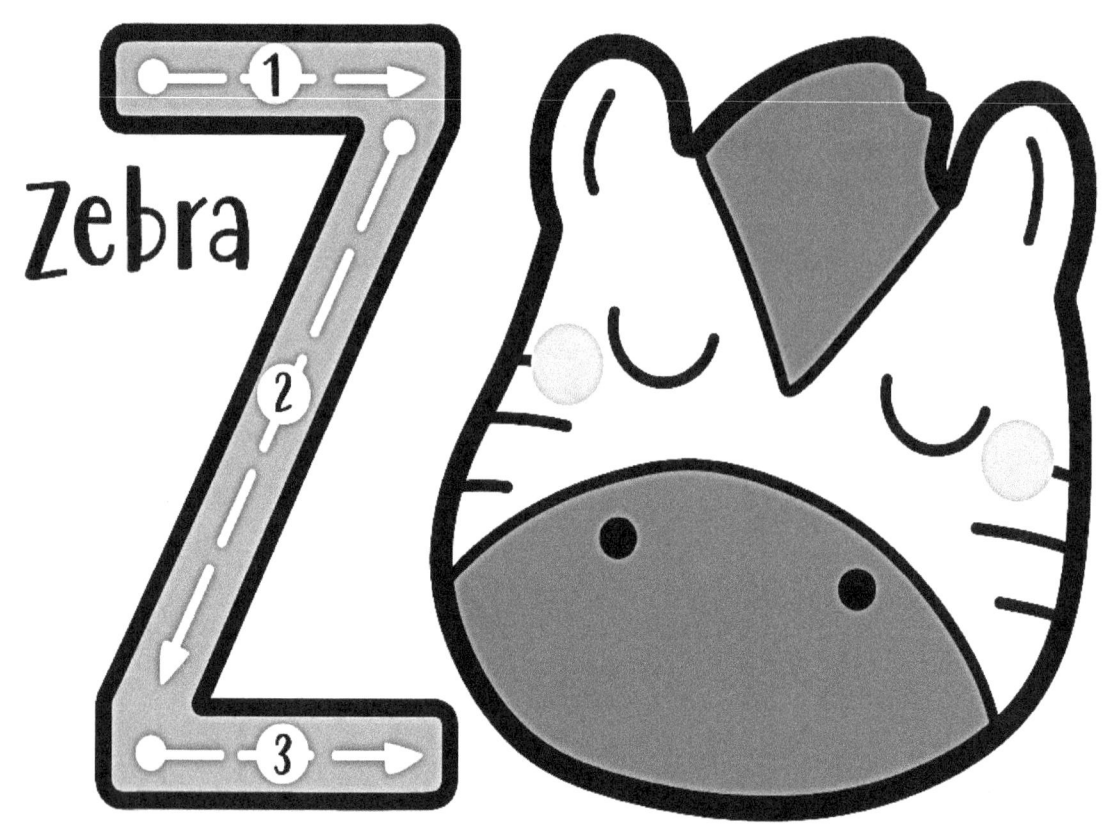

Trace & Color Letters

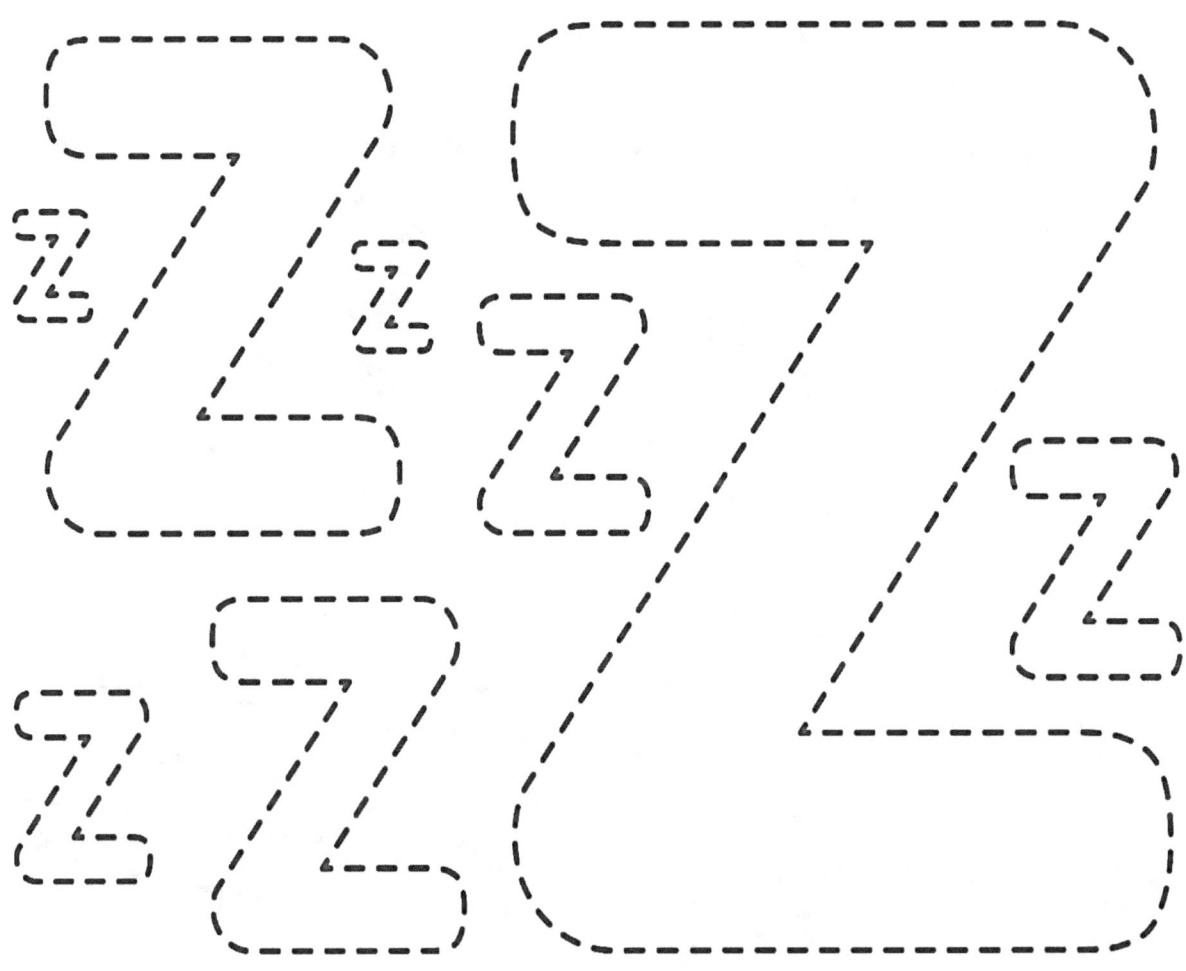

Bonus Activity

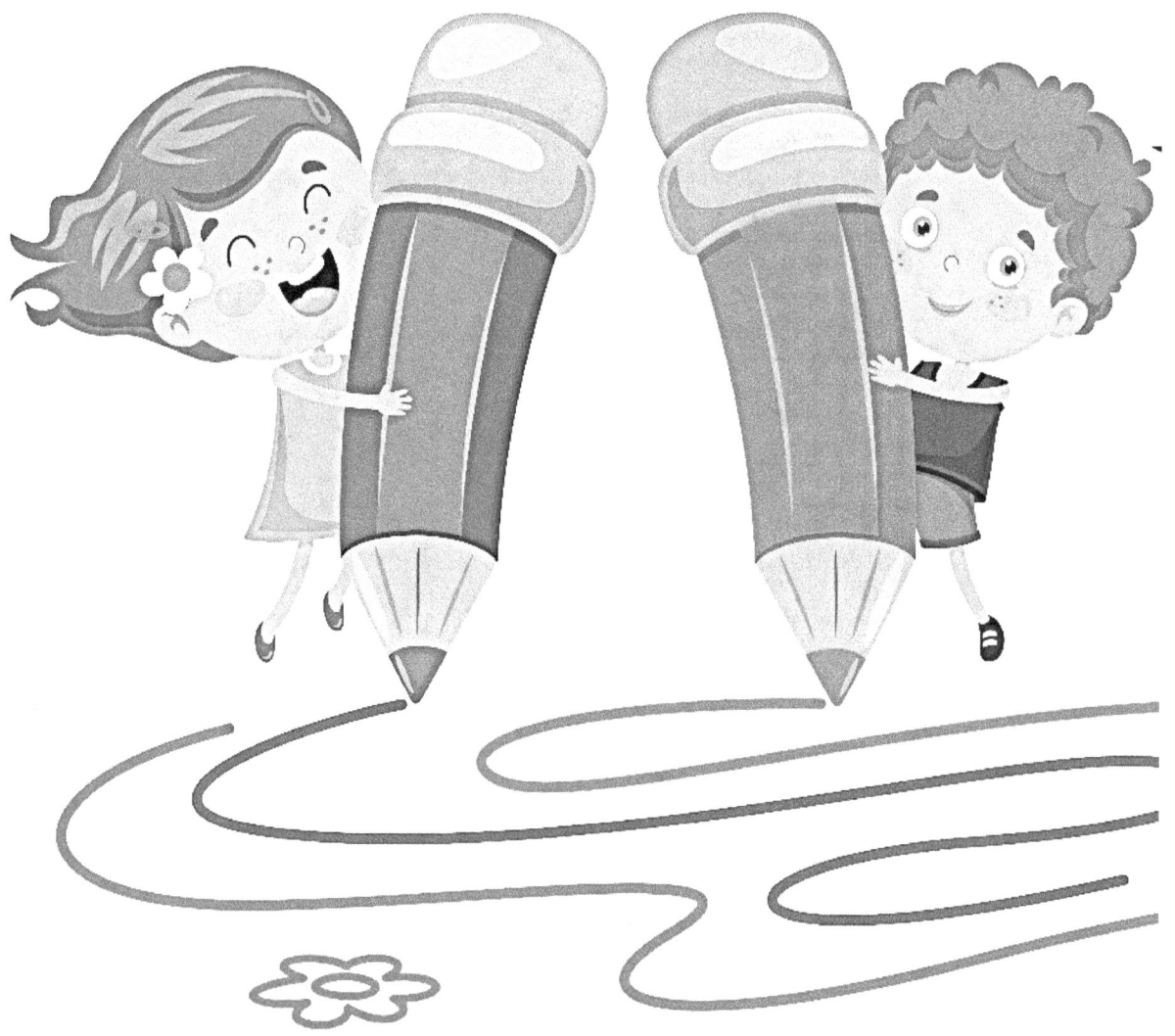

Good Job

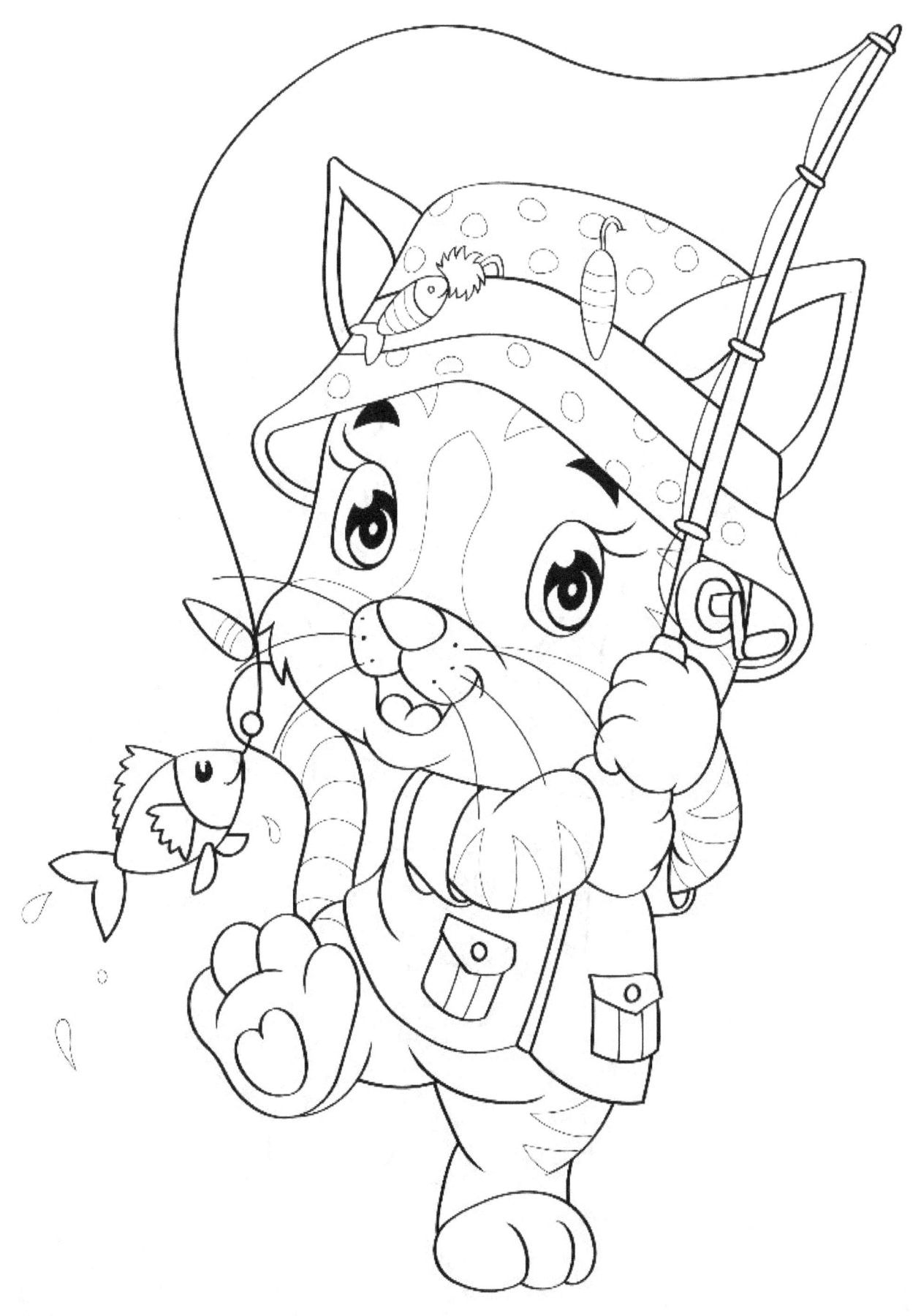

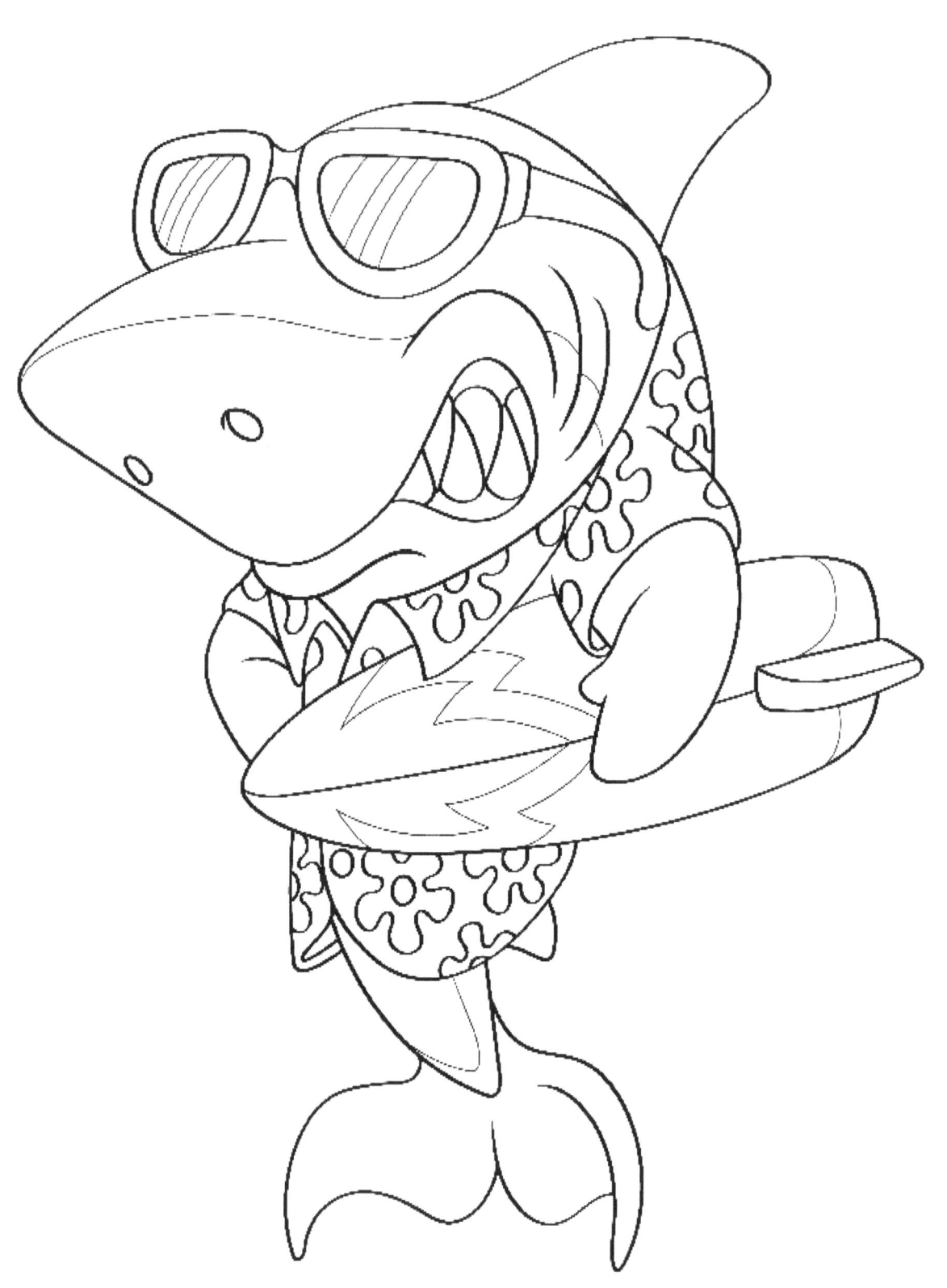

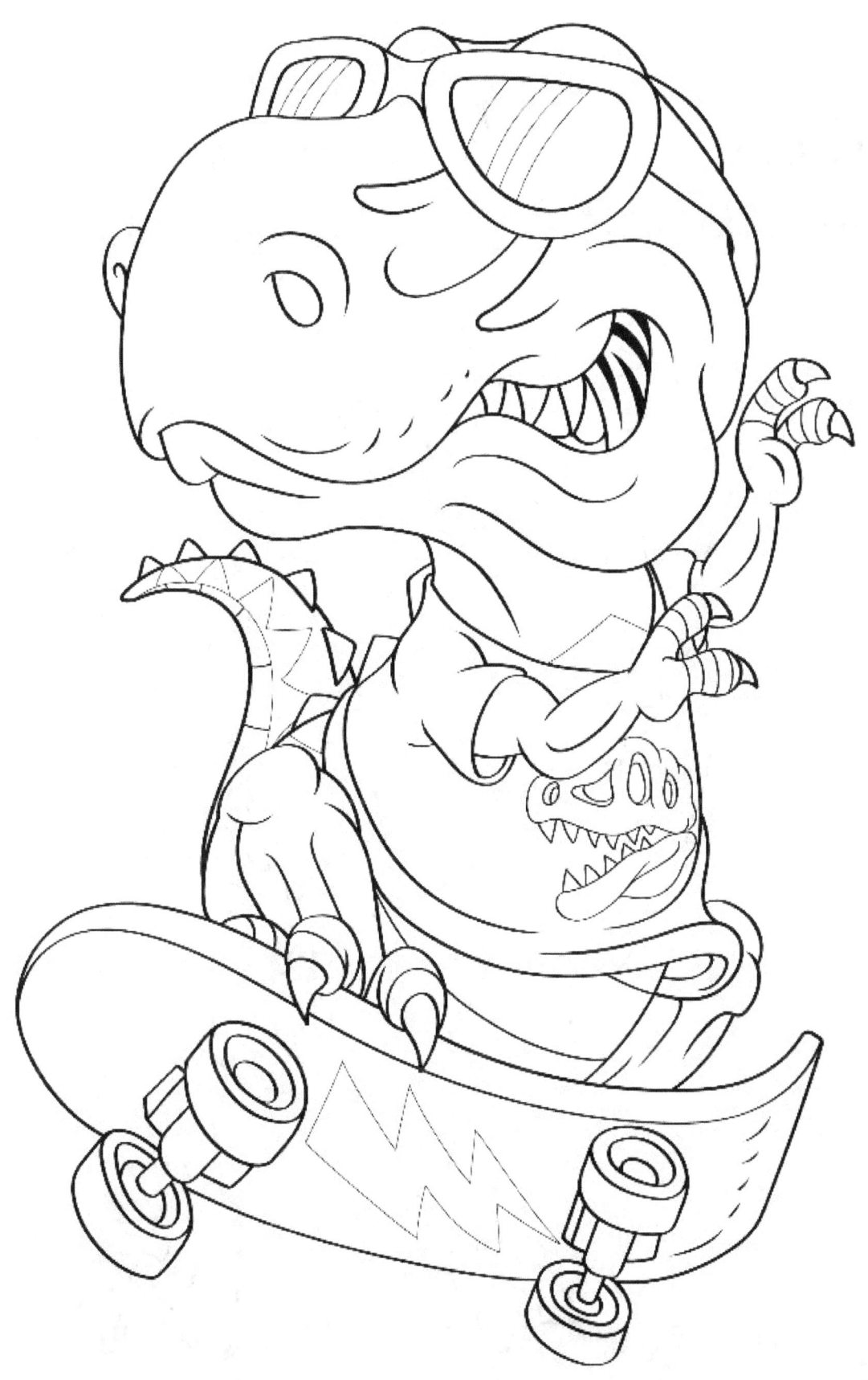

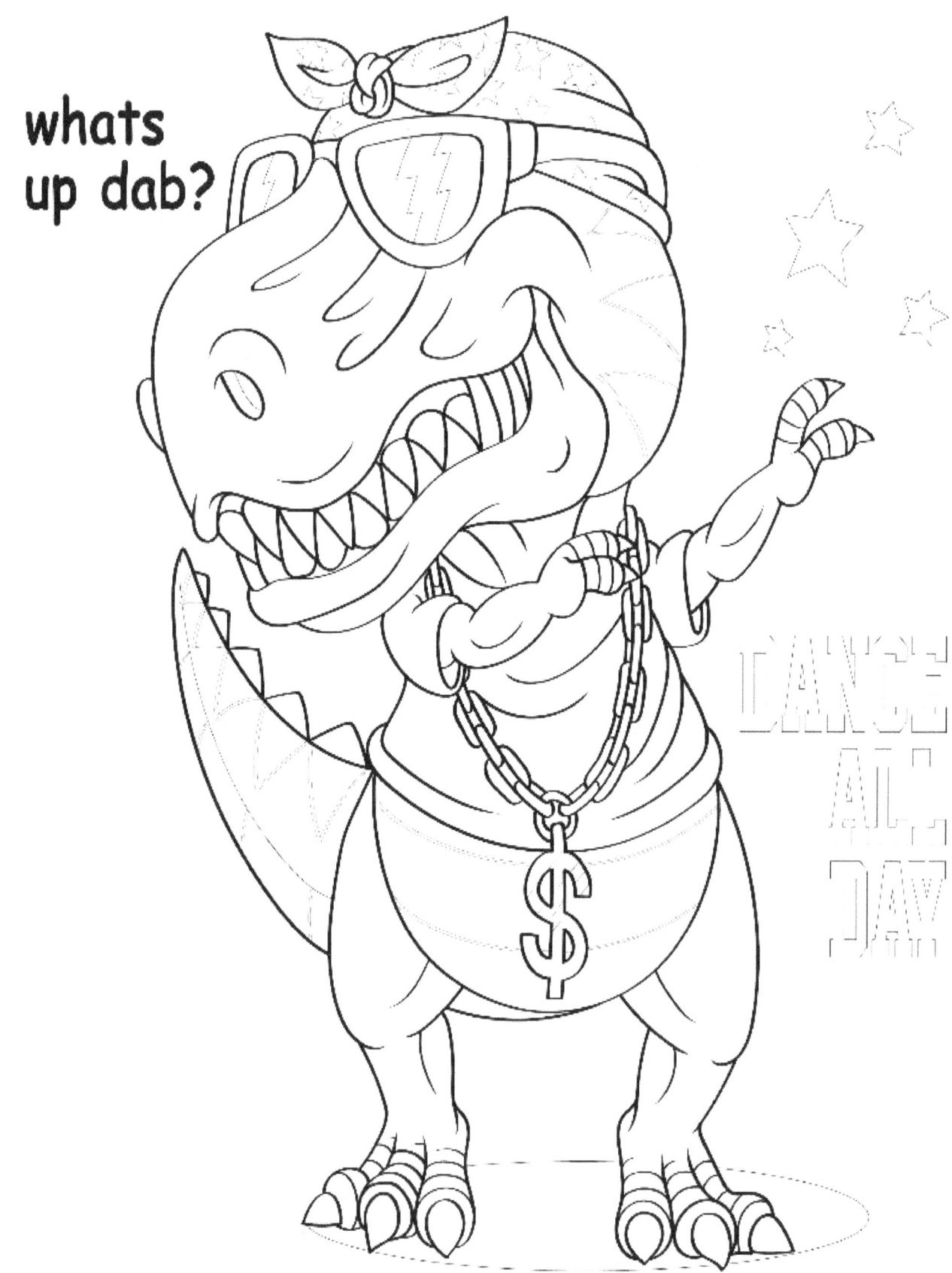

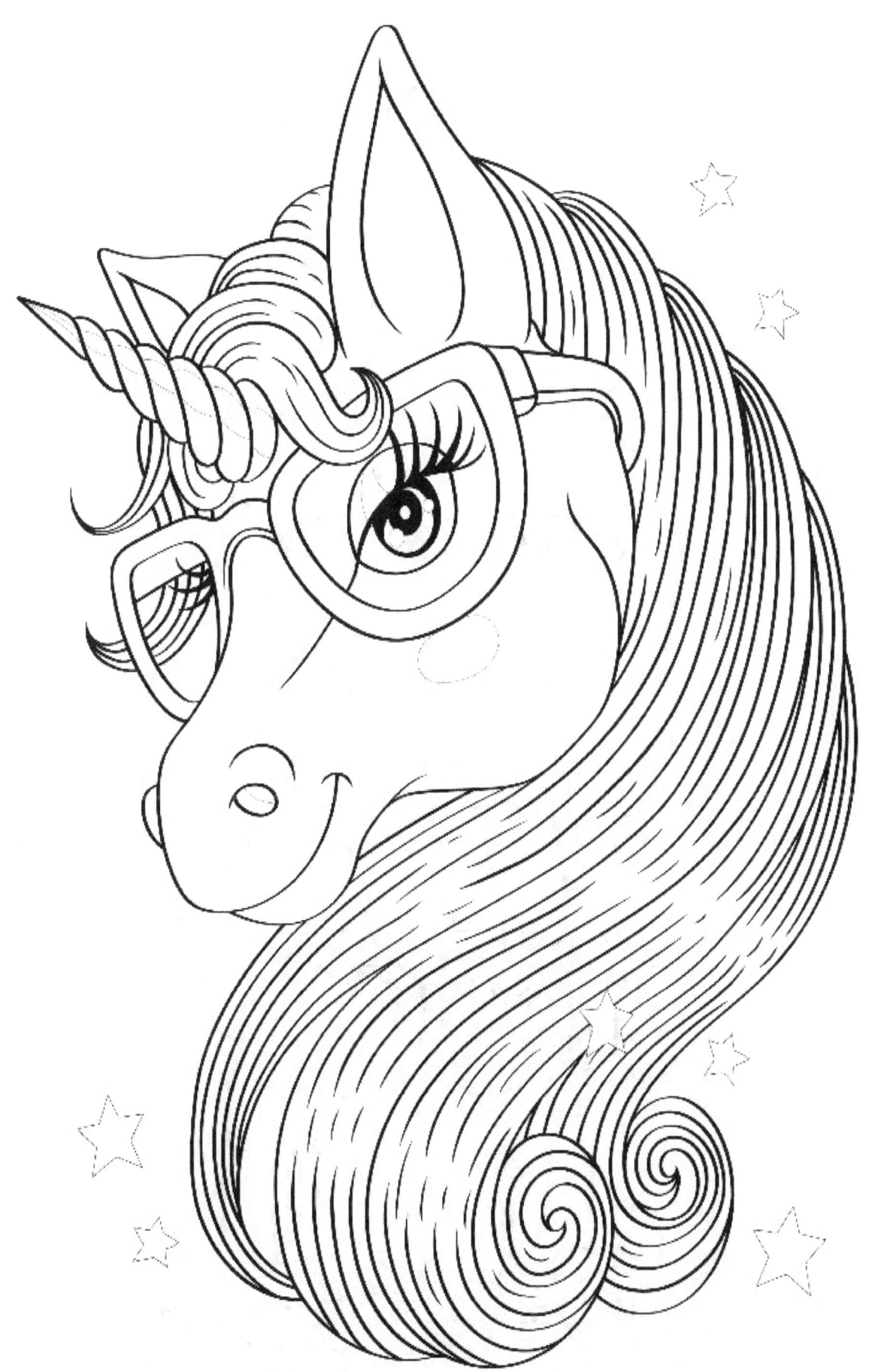

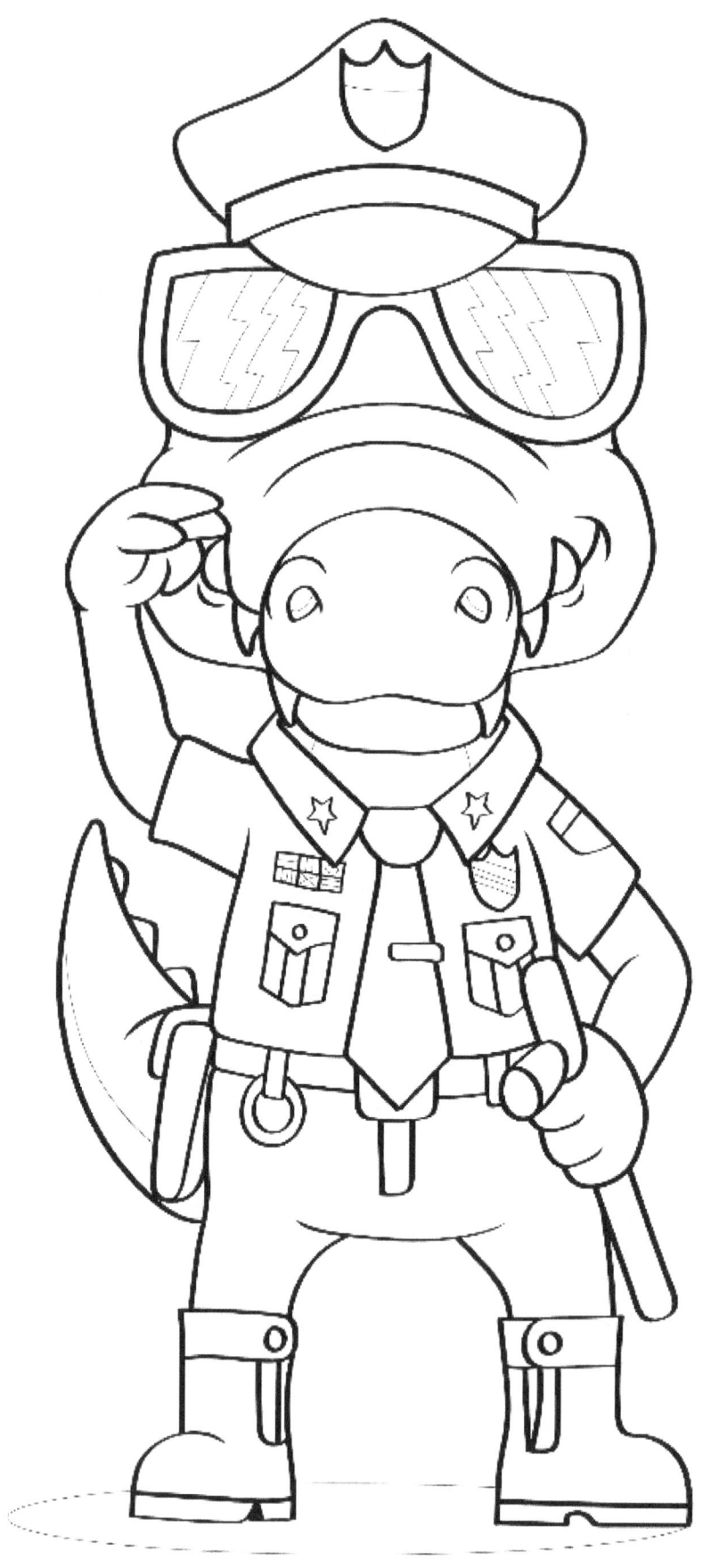

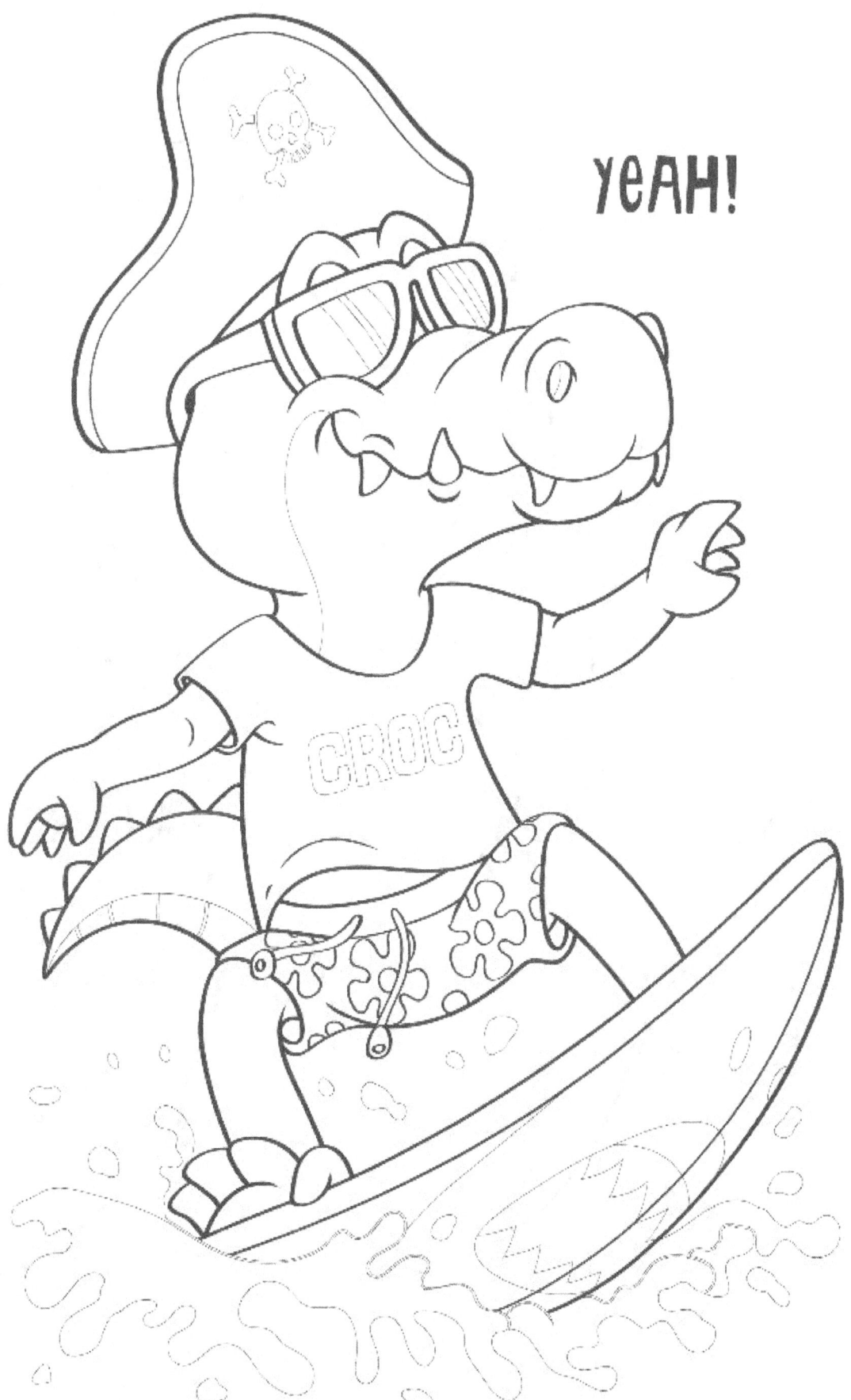

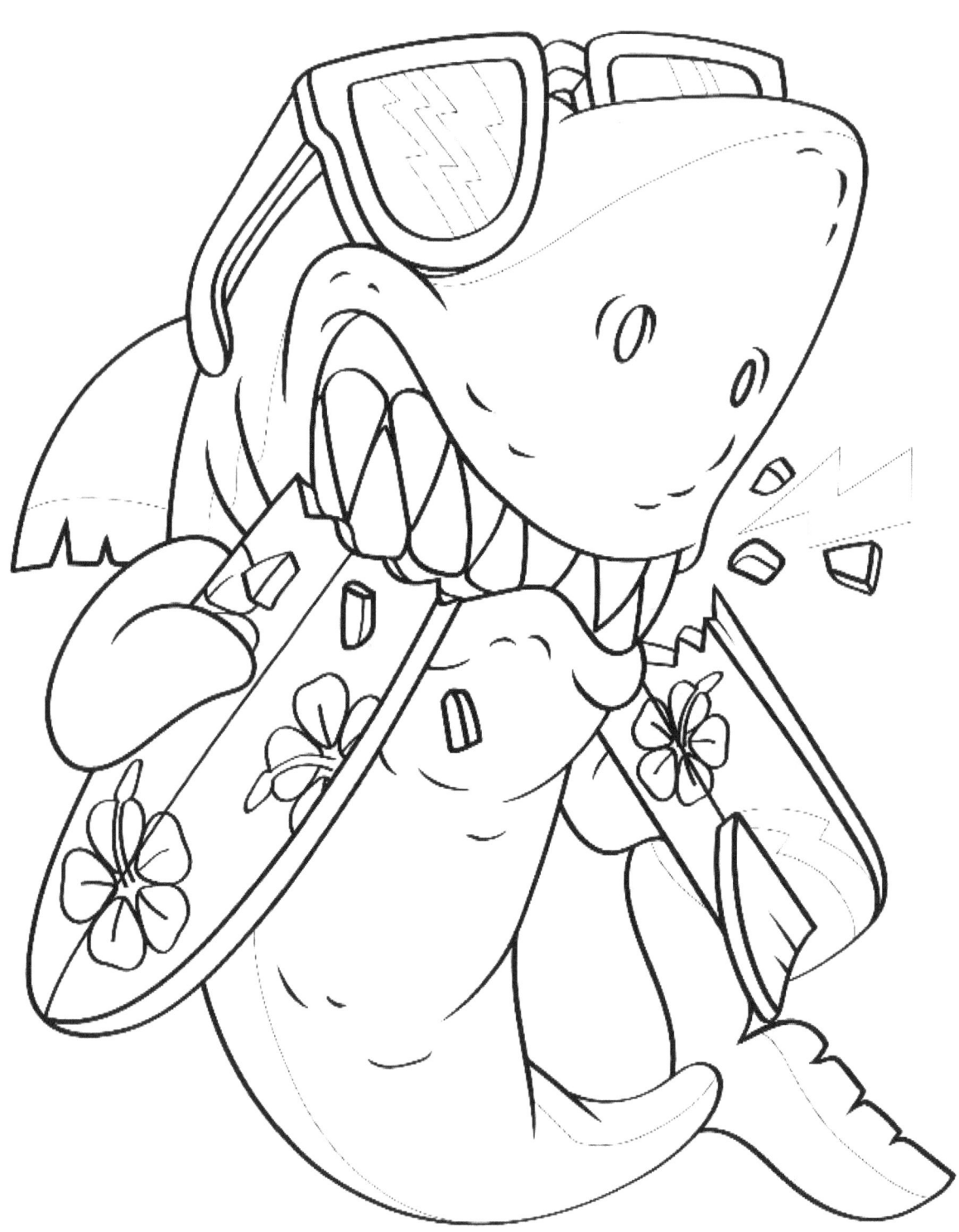

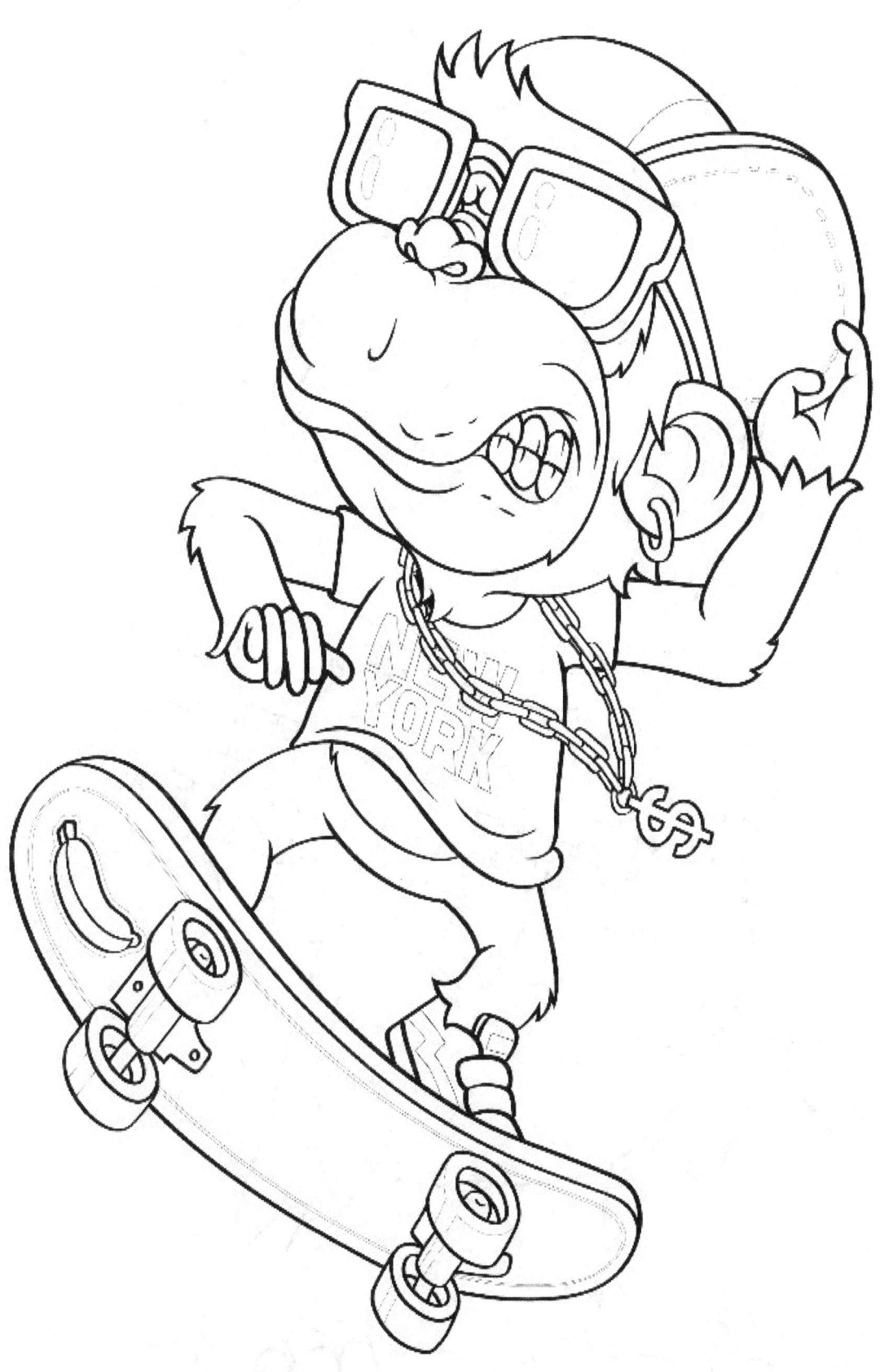

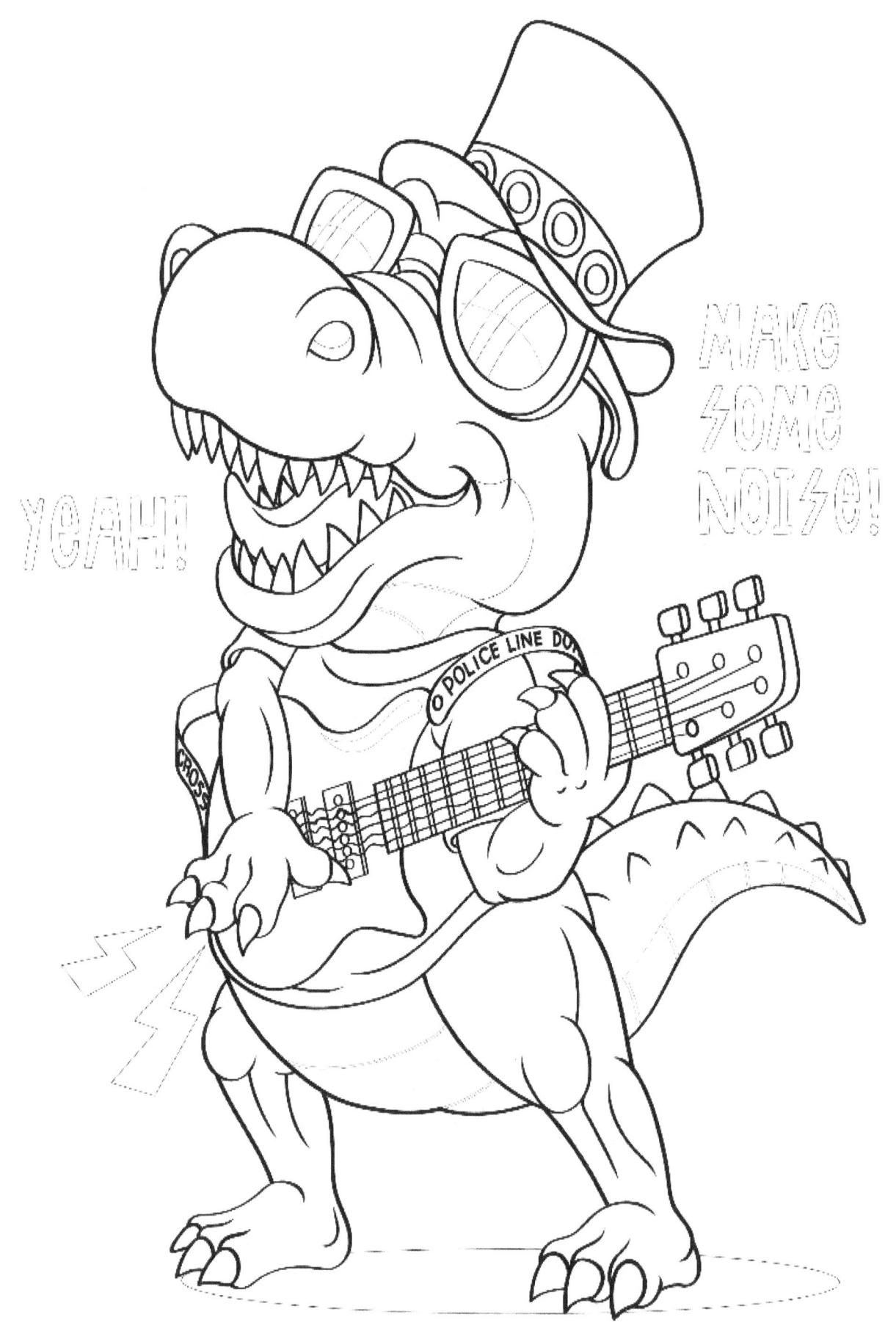

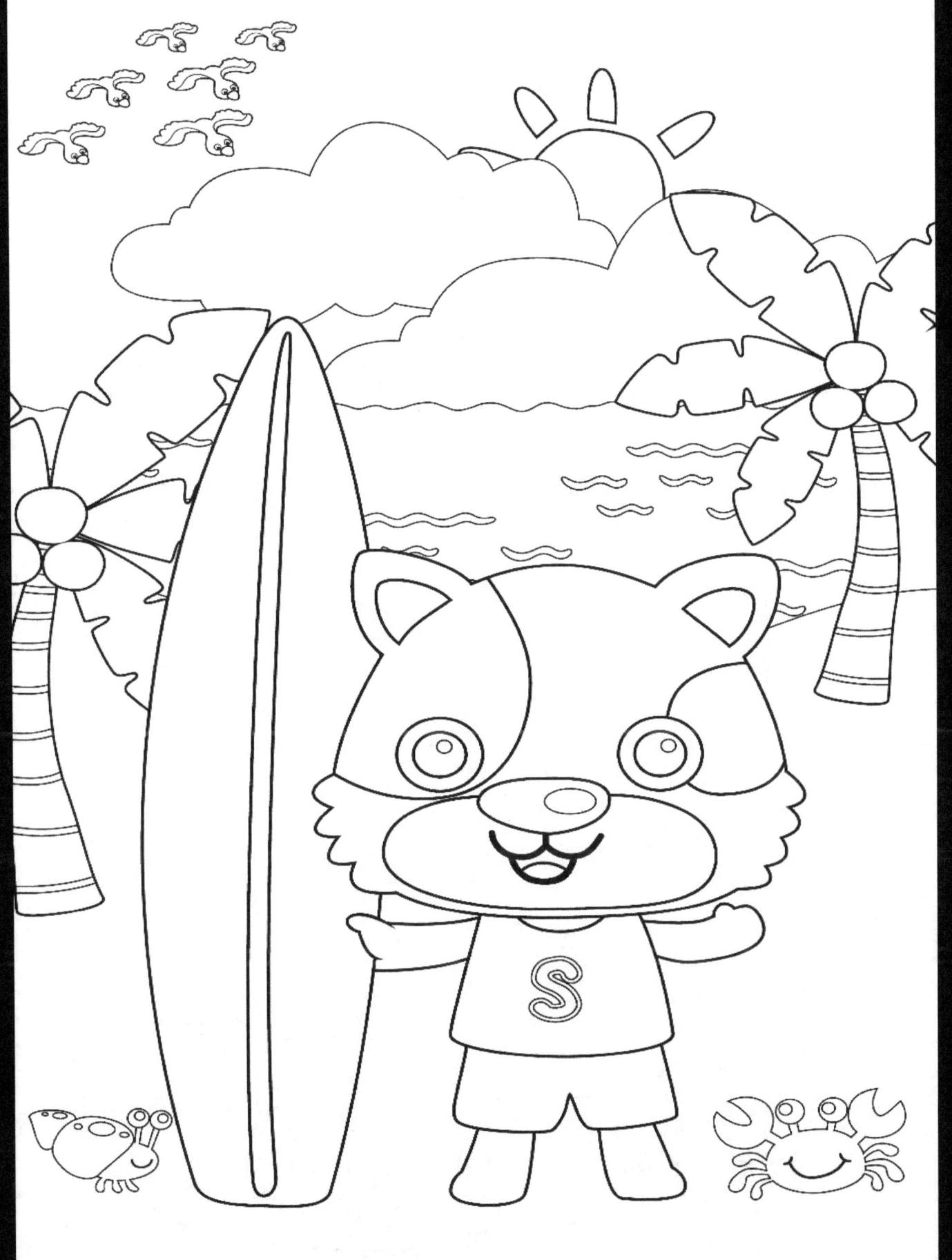

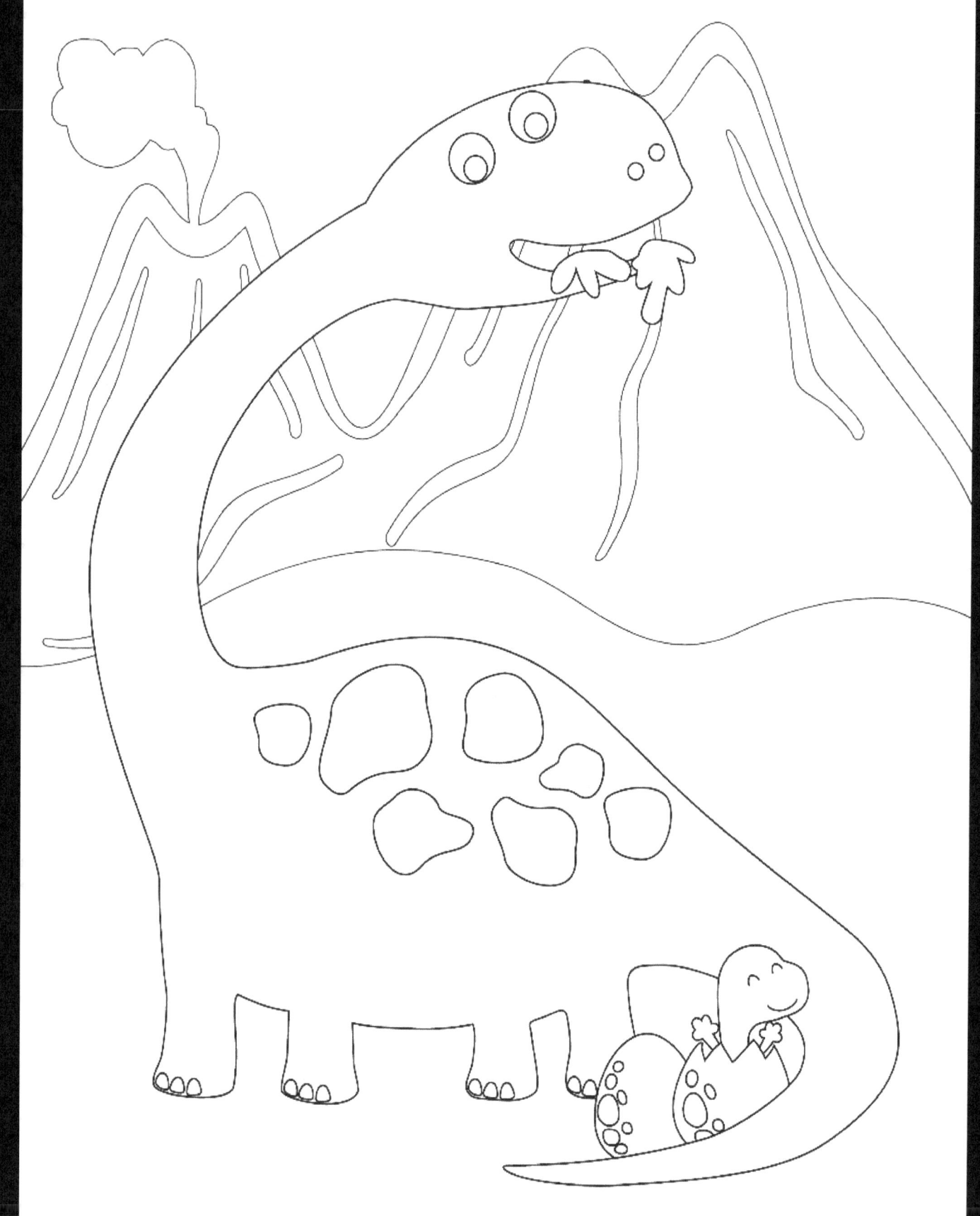

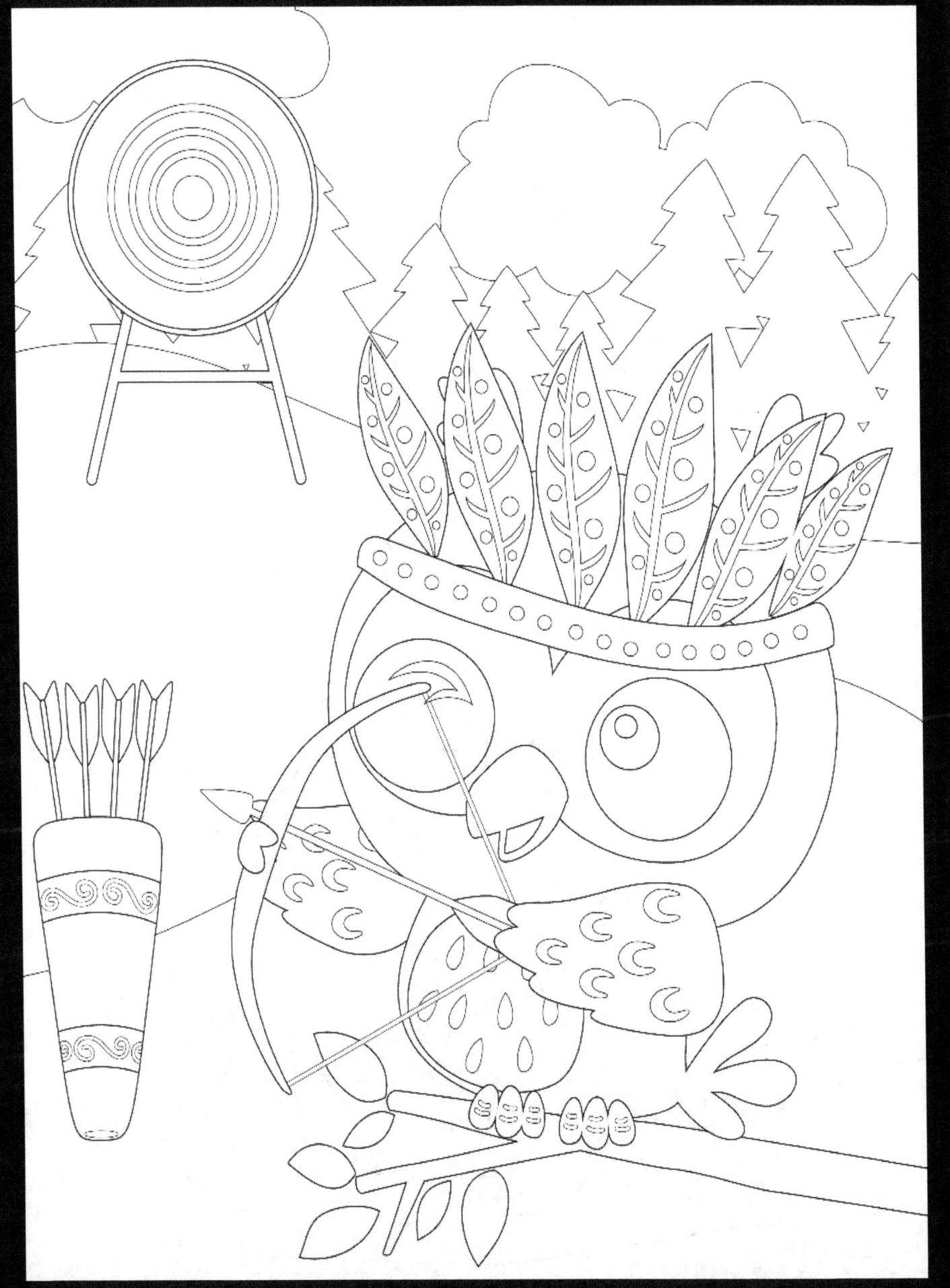

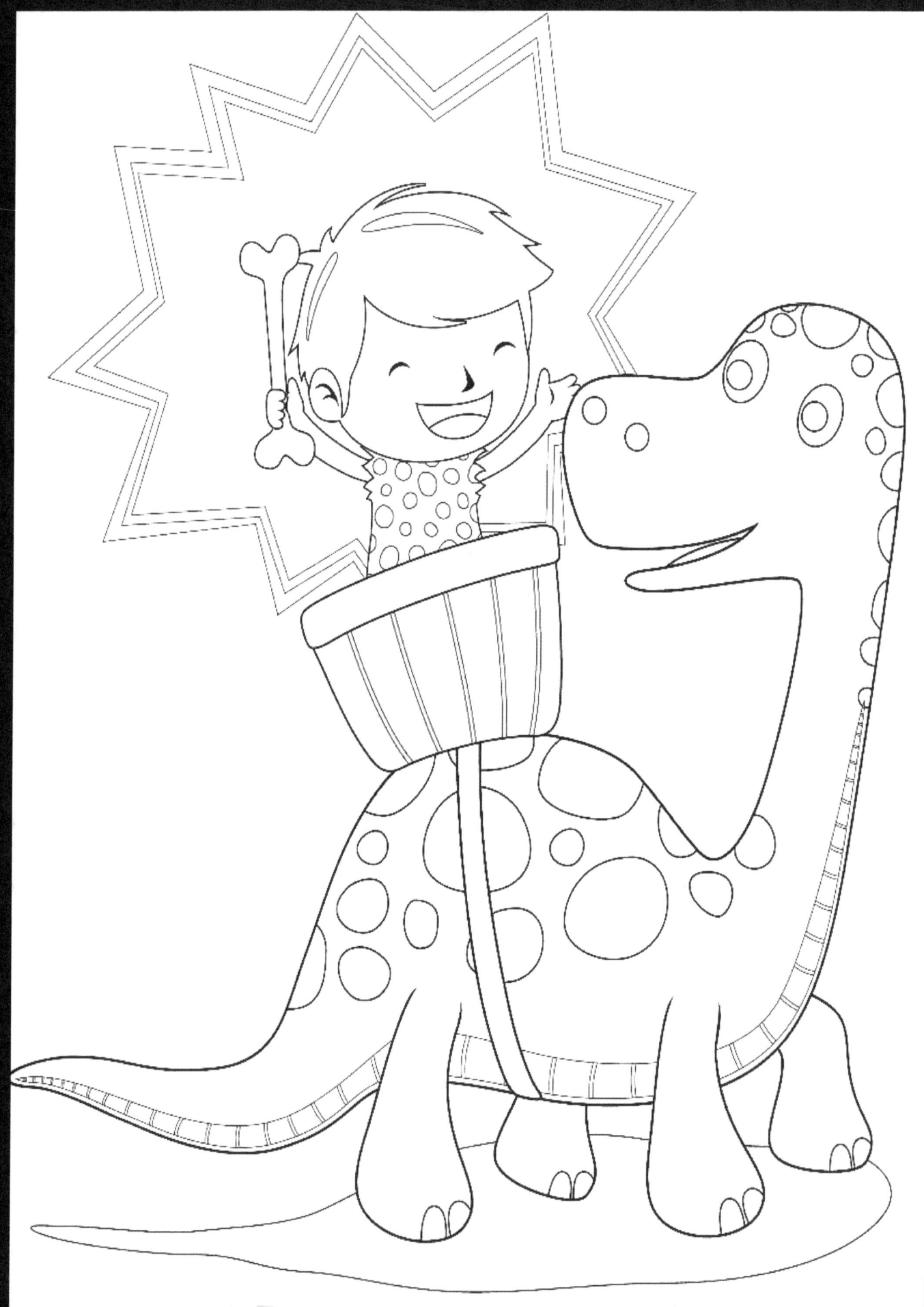

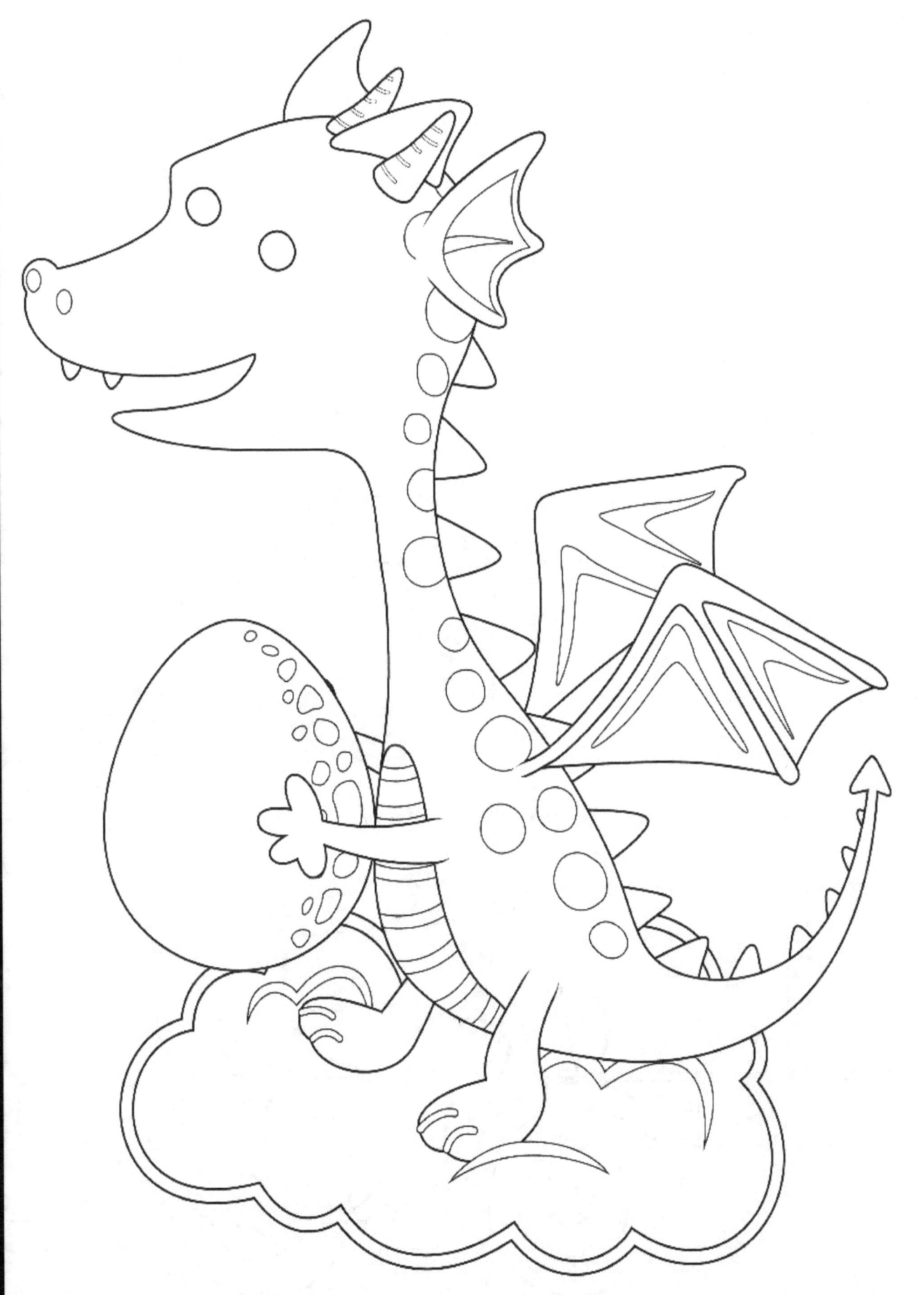

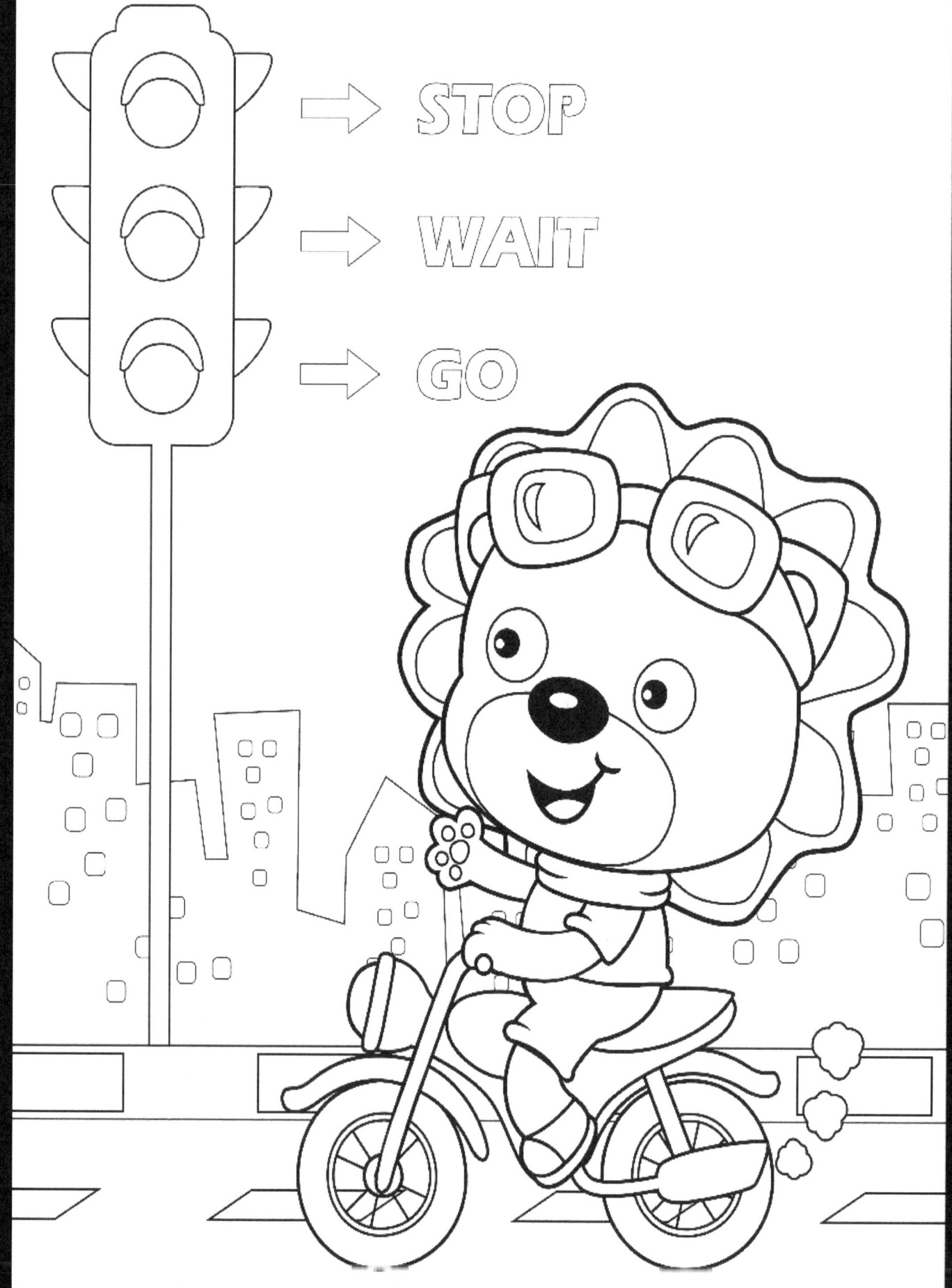

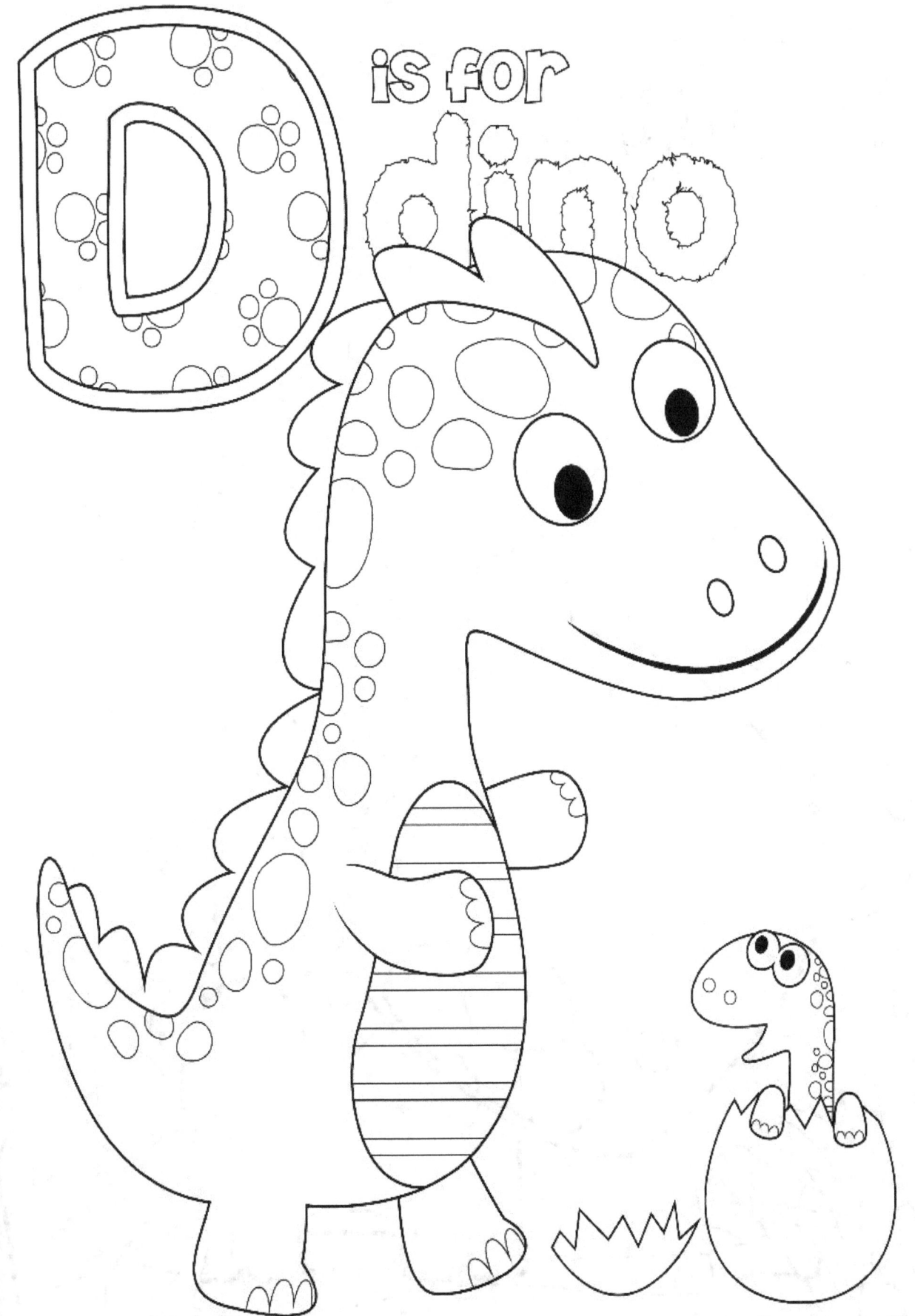

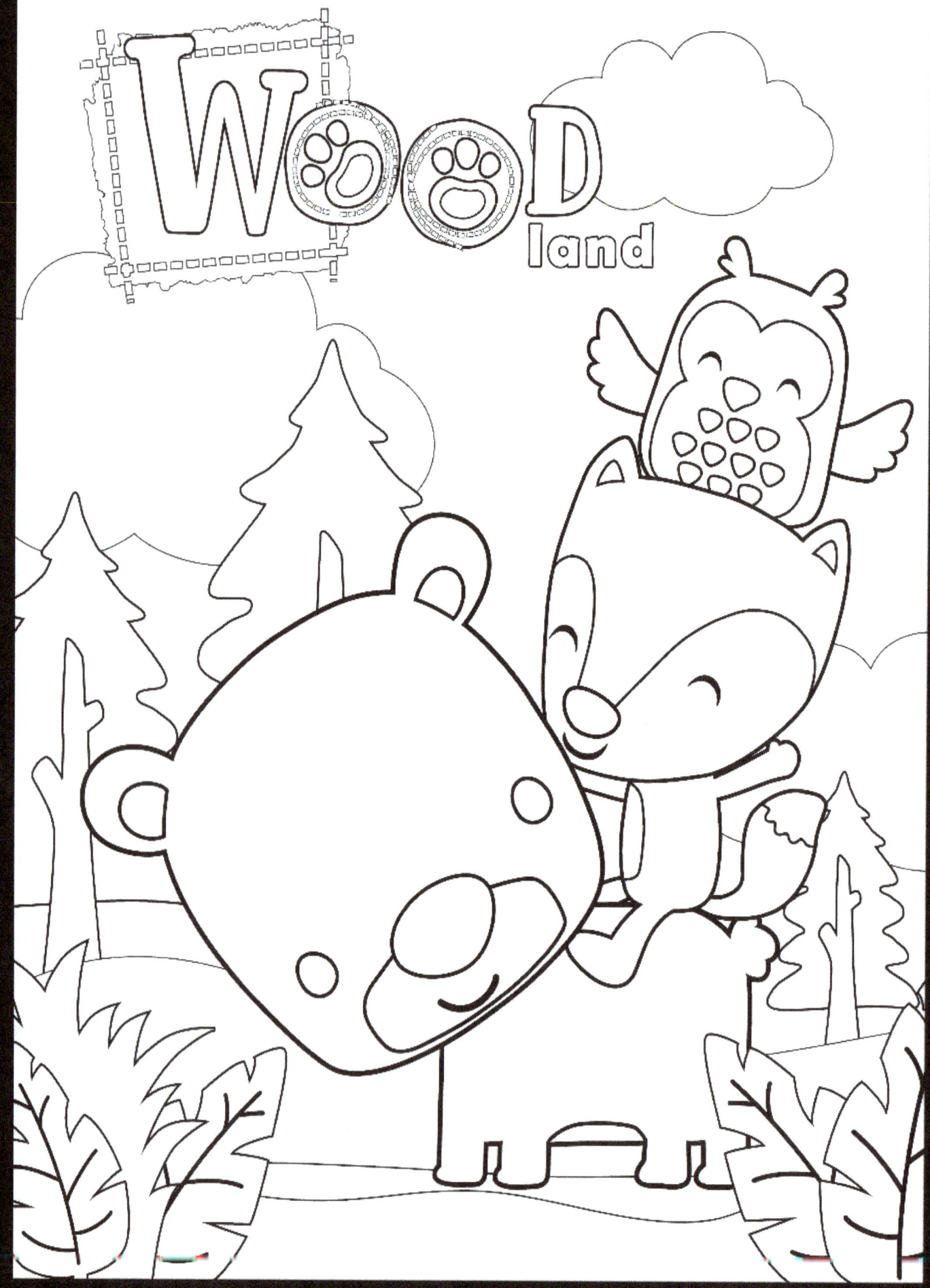

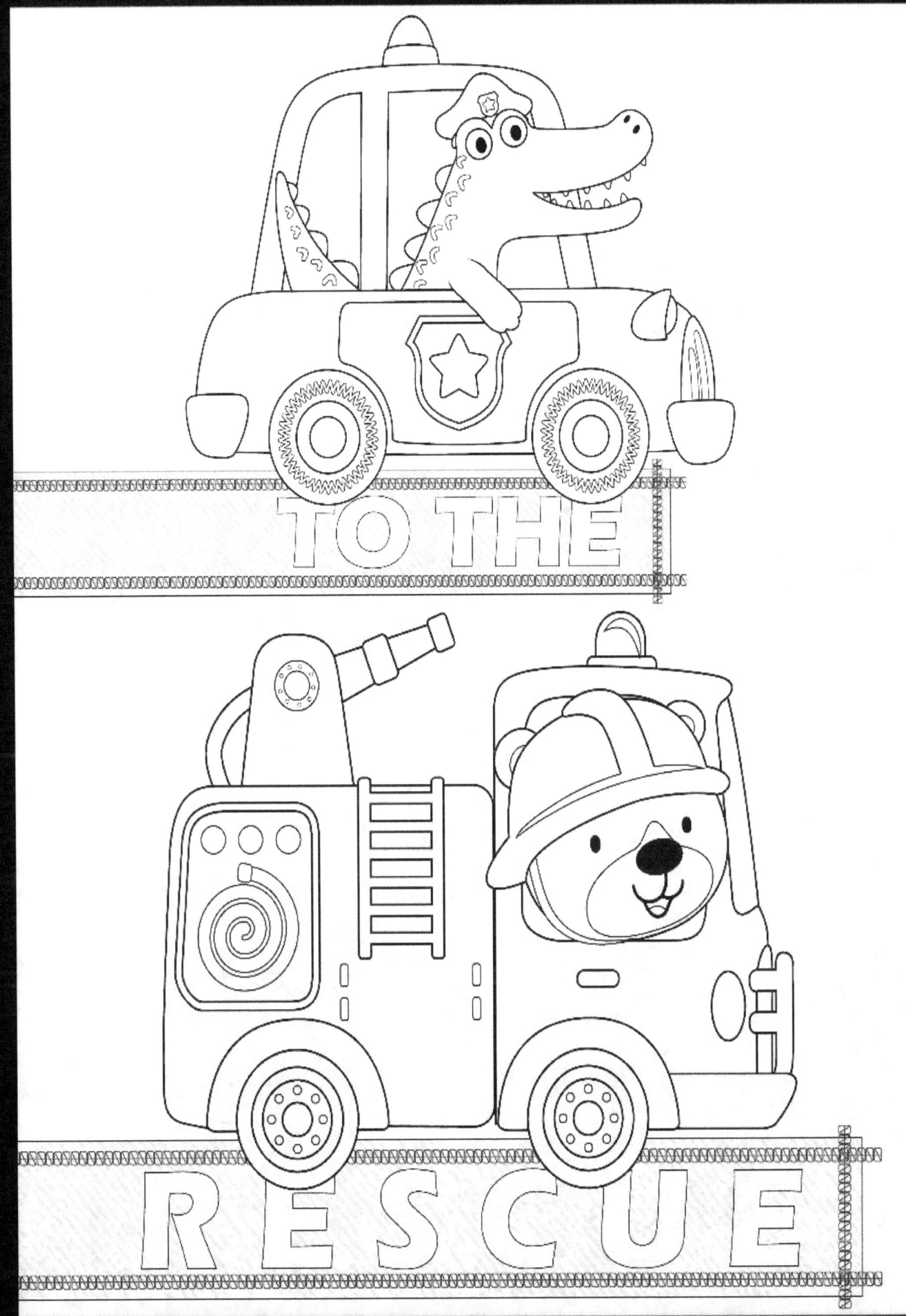

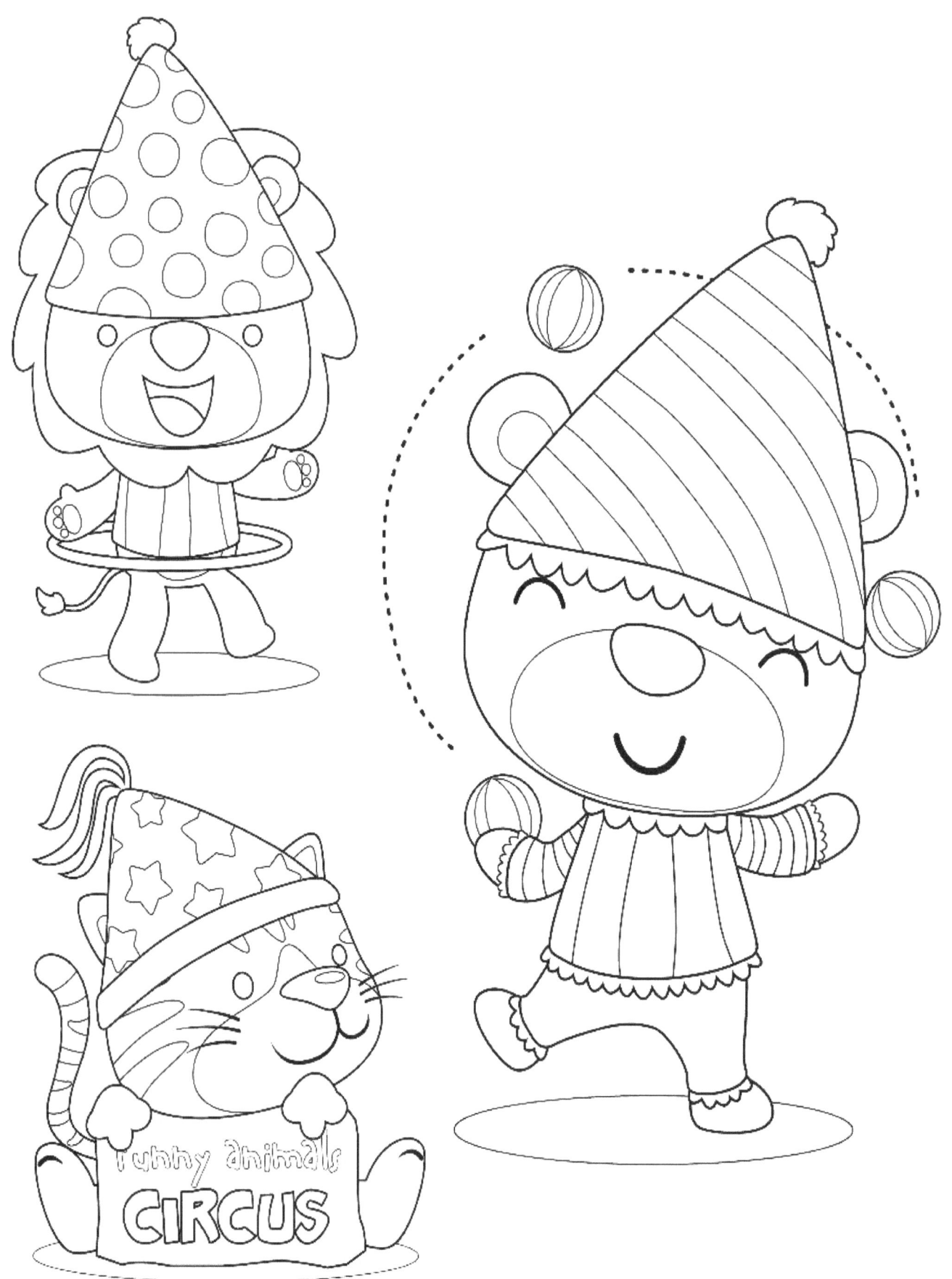

www.ingramcontent.com/pod-product-compliance
Lightning Source LLC
Chambersburg PA
CBHW080320220320

45465CB00006B/2544